# Cambridge Elements ≡

Elements in the Philosophy of Law
edited by
George Pavlakos
*University of Glasgow*
Gerald J. Postema
*University of North Carolina at Chapel Hill*
Kenneth M. Ehrenberg
*University of Surrey*

# THE MORAL PREREQUISITES OF THE CRIMINAL LAW

## *Legal Moralism and the Problem of* Mala Prohibita

Ambrose Y. K. Lee
*School of Law, University of Surrey*
Alexander F. Sarch
*School of Law, University of Surrey*

CAMBRIDGE
UNIVERSITY PRESS

Shaftesbury Road, Cambridge CB2 8EA, United Kingdom

One Liberty Plaza, 20th Floor, New York, NY 10006, USA

477 Williamstown Road, Port Melbourne, VIC 3207, Australia

314–321, 3rd Floor, Plot 3, Splendor Forum, Jasola District Centre,
New Delhi – 110025, India

103 Penang Road, #05–06/07, Visioncrest Commercial, Singapore 238467

Cambridge University Press is part of Cambridge University Press & Assessment,
a department of the University of Cambridge.

We share the University's mission to contribute to society through the pursuit of
education, learning and research at the highest international levels of excellence.

www.cambridge.org
Information on this title: www.cambridge.org/9781009454384

DOI: 10.1017/9781009000659

First published 2023

*A catalogue record for this publication is available from the British Library*

ISBN 978-1-009-45438-4 Hardback
ISBN 978-1-009-00974-4 Paperback
ISSN 2631-5815 (online)
ISSN 2631-5807 (print)

# The Moral Prerequisites of the Criminal Law

## Legal Moralism and the Problem of *Mala Prohibita*

Elements in Philosophy of Law

DOI: 10.1017/9781009000659
First published online: September 2023

Ambrose Y. K. Lee
*School of Law, University of Surrey*

Alexander F. Sarch
*School of Law, University of Surrey*

**Author for correspondence:** Alexander F. Sarch, a.sarch@surrey.ac.uk

**Abstract:** Modern states criminalise many actions that intuitively do not seem morally wrong, particularly in the context of regulating complex industries or activities. Are mala prohibita offences of this kind fundamentally mistaken? Many criminal law scholars have thought so and argued that conduct must be morally wrong to be legitimately criminalised. This Element examines the longstanding debates about whether this idea is right, and what we would lose if we either abandoned the criminal law's close connection to morality or our use of the very useful tool of mala prohibita crimes. This Element argues that there are a range of promising arguments for reconciling mala prohibita offences with the wrongness constraint on criminalisation. Thus, it seeks to shed light on the aims of the criminal law and the moral prerequisites for legitimate criminalisation.

This Element has a video abstract, available at www.cambridge.org/lee-sarch

**Keywords:** criminalisation, legal moralism, wrongness constraint, punishment, criminal law, morality

ISBNs: 9781009454384 (HB), 9781009009744 (PB), 9781009000659 (OC)
ISSNs: 2631-5815 (online), 2631-5807 (print)

# Contents

## 1 The Problem of *Mala Prohibita*

What happens when law and morality diverge? What should you do when the law requires doing something you seem to have no moral reason to do – that, for all you can see, would not be morally wrong to refuse to do? Would it be fair for the law to punish you in such a case when it is reasonable for you to be confident that you have done nothing morally wrong and much of the public would agree? Or would you feel unfairly treated if you are punished for doing something that morality appears not to prohibit but which political actors decided to criminalise anyway? When the requirements of the law seem not to be underpinned by the precepts of morality, which one takes precedence and what does this mean for the legitimacy of the criminal laws passed in the absence of clear moral grounding?

These are big questions, which this Element aims to shed light on. To sharpen the issue, consider Rhea, a highly trained chemist with several decades' experience disposing of hazardous waste for large mining companies. She now heads up the waste disposal unit at Big Bore Inc. As a hard-nosed scientist, she is impatient with red tape and paperwork she deems pointless.

The company begins disposing of a new type of regulated waste – 'stinkum' – which causes skin burns and cancer if not handled properly but becomes inert and harmless if disposed of using the right chemical processes. Given its dangers, stinkum disposal requires a permit. It is (let us suppose) covered by the US Resource Conservation and Recovery Act, which makes it a crime to knowingly dispose of a listed form of hazardous waste without a permit – punishable by up to five years in prison plus fines of up to $50,000 per day of violation.[1]

However, Rhea knows as well as anyone how to safely dispose of stinkum, as she has designed and implemented such disposal processes many times before. Given her disdain for bureaucracy, she does not go through the laborious process of getting the required permit before commencing the disposal process – though the disposal is entirely safe and even in excess of industry standards.

Rhea has committed a crime. But has she done anything morally wrong? Perhaps not. If not, is it legitimate to punish her plausibly unobjectionable conduct? This, in a nutshell, is the puzzle posed by mala prohibita offences[2] – that is, conduct

---

[1]  42 USC § 6928(d)(2)(A).

[2]  When talking about multiple offences, we use the plural: 'mala prohibita offences' or just 'mala prohibita'. But when talking about a single offence, we use the singular: 'a malum prohibitum offence' or 'malum prohibitum conduct'.

that is not wrong in itself, but which the law nonetheless singles out and deems to be criminal. Mala prohibita offences abound in modern legal systems – often as part of regulatory schemes aimed at protecting public health or promoting trustworthy and efficient markets (as with laws requiring financial disclosures or registering securities to sell them). Looking widely at other jurisdictions, further examples might include walking on the grass, chewing gum, driving on the 'wrong' side of the road, gambling, being drunk in public, exposing one's face or ankles, and more.[3]

Because a criminal conviction conveys society's strongest condemnation, a traditional view (dubbed the 'wrongness constraint' in Section 1.2) is that we cannot properly criminalise a type of conduct unless it is morally wrong. After all, the criminal law's condemnation would be neither deserved nor accurate unless the conduct condemned *really is* morally wrong. So how do we make sense of mala prohibita offences, given that they are not in themselves morally wrong? Wouldn't criminalising them when not morally wrong violate the wrongness constraint, which is built into traditional views of the criminal law's aims and proper scope?

Given that Rhea has not done anything inherently dangerous, risky or particularly irresponsible, one might wonder how it can be legitimate to deem her seemingly unobjectionable conduct to be criminal. If she has not done anything plausibly morally wrong, then the wrongness constraint would preclude the criminalisation and punishment of what she did. Cases like this are bound to come up regularly, and so the challenge is to explain how the many mala prohibita offences in modern legal systems are not broadly incompatible with the wrongness constraint.

In the rest of this section, we examine more carefully what this puzzle involves and what is at stake in thinking about it. First, we take a closer look at what mala prohibita are and how they relate to other nearby concepts like proxy crimes. Then we explicate the conventional view that criminalisation requires moral wrongness, both to understand more precisely what this wrongness constraint requires and to lay out the motivations behind it. Finally, we return to the puzzle of mala prohibita and discuss what is at stake here and what kinds of solutions to it can be offered. We close by outlining how the rest of this Element is structured.

---

[3] These are illustrative examples only. For an entertaining discussion of a wide range of mala prohibita in US federal law, see Chase 2019.

## 1.1 What Are *Mala Prohibita*?

### *1.1.1* Mala In Se *versus* Mala Prohibita

Mala prohibita are to be contrasted with mala in se offences.[4] The latter are types of conduct – like murder, theft and rape – that are[5] morally wrong in themselves, or independently of the law. By contrast, mala prohibita offences (roughly) are acts that have been declared crimes although not morally wrong in themselves; rather, if they are wrongful at all, this is because the law has prohibited them.[6]

For example, it is a crime in the United States for a person engaged in trade to fail to report cash transactions over \$10,000 to the tax authorities.[7] Absent a prohibition on such conduct as part of an anti-money-laundering regulatory regime, who would have thought that failing to report such a cash transaction was morally wrongful? Without the state establishing this regulatory regime, it is unlikely that any individual would have reached the conclusion of their own accord that this conduct is morally wrong. In this sense, this offence is a good example of conduct that is not mala in se (i.e. morally wrong independently of law), but rather purports to be wrongful only because it has been singled out as criminal.

---

[4] For some of the intriguing history of the malum in se versus malum prohibitum distinction, see Ristroph 2011b: 582–4. Ristroph explains that originally mala prohibita were offences the king could grant exceptions to as they were theoretically his creation, while the king could not similarly authorise the performance of mala in se offences.

[5] If you are a moral anti-realist (i.e. someone who rejects the notion of 'objective' or mind-independent moral truths), you can replace 'are' in the above sentence with 'are considered to be'. For present purposes, we set aside the thorny metaethical debate between moral realism and anti-realism. We will generally write as if moral realism is true, but this is just a simplifying assumption. Our arguments and conclusions can be recast to fit within anti-realist views by redescribing our talk of what morality requires or prohibits, or is supported by moral reasons, and so on, as claims about what is generally regarded in the relevant society as morally required, prohibited or supported by moral reasons. Thus, we join the many criminal law theorists who want their conclusions about the relationship between criminal law and morality to be plausible regardless of which metaethical theory proves correct. These claims just have to be interpreted slightly differently depending on which metaethical view is adopted. (Note also that even if realism is true, there can be disagreement about which actions are morally right or wrong. The existence of objective moral facts does not entail that there will be a universal consensus about what these facts are.)

[6] For the avoidance of doubt, we do not intend the terms 'morally wrong' and 'morally wrongful' to convey any substantive difference. Some theorists distinguish these terms, but such a usage requires defence. Here we use them interchangeably.

[7] This is a combination of the following statutes: 26 USC § 6050I and 26 USC 7203. Individuals engaged in trade must use IRS Form 8300 to report such cash transactions to the IRS. Likewise, banks are required to report any cash transactions over \$10,000 for reasons related to combatting money laundering. 31 USC § 5313. It is also an offence to 'structure' such transactions into amounts below this threshold to evade the relevant requirement. 31 USC § 5324. (Note while many of our examples are drawn from US law, the theories and arguments considered here apply broadly to any modern jurisdiction, though especially common law jurisdictions.)

One way of understanding this distinction[8] is to contrast mala in se with mala prohibita by saying the former covers conduct that is pre-legally wrongful while the latter covers conduct which is not pre-legally wrongful.[9] However, this temporal definition faces difficulties. It is not always important what was or would have been wrongful before the relevant laws were passed. Perhaps the relevant conduct was impossible prior to the relevant law and was only brought into existence with the passage of the statute in question. For example, prior to the laws establishing the requirements for submitting individual income tax returns, and the associated criminal penalties for lying on the required tax forms – such as Form 1040 in the United States – it would not have been possible to commit the particular offence of lying on Form 1040, and so it would not have been pre-legally wrongful. Nonetheless, this does not mean that lying on the required tax form is a malum prohibitum. Lying – particularly on a solemn official statement to the government – is plausibly malum in se. The new laws here merely created a new instance of something that was already morally wrong.

So, in understanding what a malum prohibitum offence is, what is important to focus on is not what conduct would have been wrongful or not wrongful *prior* to the passage of the relevant law (or the establishment of a legal system in general), but rather on whether the conduct is wrong in itself independently of what the law says. If the existence or operation of law merely makes an incidental contribution to explaining why the conduct would be wrongful, as in fleshing out or making more concrete the details about how an independently existing wrong can be committed in a modern context (as with the 1040 tax form), this does not detract from thinking that the conduct is malum in se. This is why adding mere 'jurisdictional' elements to a crime (for example, the require-ment that wire, radio or TV communications were used to commit a fraud for it to violate 18 USC § 1343) does not change the offence from malum in se to malum prohibitum. The core of the conduct is still malum in se, despite the addition of jurisdictional elements. The law is not the substance of the explan-ation of why that conduct is wrongful; rather, it is incidental to this explanation. By contrast, when the law aims to make a piece of otherwise innocent conduct wrongful *by declaring it to be so* (as when the law criminalises engaging in a given activity without obtaining a necessary licence), then this is a strong indicator that the conduct is malum prohibitum. Thus, when the law itself is essentially involved in the substantive explanation of why the conduct is putatively wrong (i.e. why the conduct at least purports to be appropriate for

---

[8]  For another interesting but non-mainstream way of construing the distinction, see Dimock 2016.

[9]  For discussion of related issues, see note 30.

criminal punishment), then this is a good indicator that the conduct is malum prohibitum.[10] To summarise:

- Conduct is **malum in se** if it is morally wrong independently of the law not thanks to the existence, content or operation of the law.
- Conduct is **malum prohibitum** if it is not morally wrong independently of the law, but rather the existence, content or operation of the law is substantially and ineliminably (not merely incidentally) involved in explaining why this conduct is putatively wrong (i.e. is seen from the law's point of view as the sort of moral wrong that would be appropriate for criminalisation and punishment).

Youngjae Lee suggests it can be helpful to distinguish mala in se from mala prohibita components of a given offence (Lee 2021: 228). For example, if one drives dangerously over the speed limit, then the dangerous driving component of the conduct may be malum in se while the component consisting of exceeding the speed limit may be malum prohibitum.

While an illuminating suggestion, this approach also raises difficult questions about act individuation. For example, in an act of driving dangerously over the speed limit, there may seem to be simply two overlapping offences here – driving dangerously and driving over the speed limit – one that is malum in se and the other malum prohibitum. The same conduct may satisfy the elements of multiple distinct crimes, after all, and one can be punishable for all of them if proven beyond a reasonable doubt.

To avoid such complications, we will focus, where possible, on clear-cut cases of either malum prohibitum or malum in se conduct. So as not to become embroiled in questions of taxonomy, we largely side-step offences that might seem to contain an equal mix of malum in se and malum prohibitum elements and instead aim to focus on offences that more clearly fall on one side or the other of the line between malum in se and malum prohibitum. Moreover, we refer to crimes that have substantial malum prohibitum components simply as 'mala prohibita offences'.

---

[10] Note that we describe mala prohibita as conduct that 'purports to be wrongful' or 'is putatively wrongful' because we mean to leave it an open question whether the conduct at issue actually is wrongful on closer inspection or not. When an act type is criminalised, it is plausible that at least in the view of the legislators passing the statute – or more abstractly, from the point of view of the law – the conduct is taken to be morally wrongful. However, both the law and the legislators behind it may of course be mistaken. The conduct may on reflection turn out not to be wrongful at all. We do not want to pre-judge matters by defining malum prohibitum conduct as that which *really is* wrongful only because prohibited or because of the operation of law. Rather, we say that it is conduct that at least *purports* to be wrongful only because of the law (and not independently thereof).

### 1.1.2 Distinguishing Mala Prohibita *from Related Concepts*

There are several other partially overlapping concepts in the neighbourhood of mala prohibita, but these are nonetheless distinct and should be kept separate.

**Proxy crimes**. These are crimes that punish some explicitly defined offence conduct (the proxy) *as the means* to combatting some other conduct (the target conduct) that the legislature is actually interested in combatting, but which is more difficult to detect and prosecute. This legislative strategy is generally chosen because the proxy conduct is seen as correlating with or being closely connected to the target conduct, but is easier to identify and prosecute than the target conduct.[11] For example, if the legislature wishes to combat money laundering (itself as a means to combatting the criminal activity that generates the money to be laundered), it may be insufficient to simply make money laundering a crime directly and leave it at that. After all, money laundering tends to occur in secretive contexts that are covered up and intermingled with legitimate income streams (think of the car wash in *Breaking Bad* or the print shop in *The Wire*), and thus can be difficult to detect. Accordingly, the legislature may find it beneficial to also battle money laundering by criminalising other types of conduct that are more easily detected and tend to correlate with or provide red flags of money-laundering activity – such as failing to report large cash transactions or other suspicious activities.

While proxy crimes might often be mala prohibita, they need not be. For example, while failing to report a cash transaction over $10,000 might be both malum prohibitum and a proxy crime for money laundering, other crimes that are more plausibly mala in se – like evading tax reporting obligations or submitting a misleading disclosure to the regulators – might also be proxies for money laundering (and criminalised in part for that reason). Thus, the notion of a proxy crime is distinct from a malum prohibitum, even if many crimes can exemplify both.[12]

**Regulatory offences**. Regulatory offences are part of a statutory scheme aimed at regulating some profession, activity or domain of life – from public health and safety to financial markets to the different aspects of the environment (such as waste disposal or emissions). Regulatory offences can of course be proxy crimes, though they need not be. For example, licensing requirements (e.g. the one Rhea faced in our earlier example) frequently figure into regulatory

---

[11] For more on proxy crimes, see Lee 2022b.

[12] While inchoate offences – like attempt or conspiracy – could likewise be supported by the desire to make it easier for prosecutors to secure convictions and increase the criminal law's deterrent effect, inchoate offences still plainly are distinct from mala prohibita. The inchoate crime of, say, attempted murder is a core malum in se offence.

schemes, but the failure to obtain a required licence to engage in some regulated activity is not necessarily a proxy crime. Regulatory offences likewise can often be mala prohibita – like failing to obtain a required licence – but they can also be mala in se, as with environmental crimes that consist in releasing or disposing of waste in ways that cause harm.

**Over-broad offences.** With offences of this kind (sometimes also called 'prophylactic crimes'), the statutory text defines a certain type of conduct as a crime although a substantial proportion of the act tokens meeting the statutory definition are not wrongful or culpable in ways that merit punishment (or the specified amount of punishment) – even after all available affirmative defences (justifications and excuses) are taken into consideration. Thus, over-broad offences are plausibly unjust in imposing criminal penalties in a wider swath of cases than are actually warranted based on the desert of the offender. The overbreadth mentioned here is relative to the class of cases in which the offender actually deserves the amount of punishment imposed.

For example, the preparatory offences in the UK Terrorism Act 2000 have been criticised as over-broad (Simester 2012). Notoriously, section 57 of the Act makes it a crime to possess 'an article in circumstances which give rise to a reasonable suspicion that his possession is for a purpose connected with the commission, preparation or instigation of an act of terrorism'. This offence covers a wide swath of conduct that is unlikely to be culpable, particularly in circumstances where one innocently interacts with individuals who the authorities believe to be engaged in terrorist activities – perhaps especially parents or friends. Thus, if Jessica possesses a box of tools that she plans to give her son, then if the son actually is planning an act of terrorism, she will have committed an offence – even though she may have only had vague concerns about his activities given that he hangs around with shady characters. The circumstances here might provide the authorities with a *reasonable suspicion* that Jessica had the purpose to aid a terrorist act. This is all that is required for her to be liable for the section 57 offence, even when *ex hypothesi* Jessica did not have any such purpose. It seems implausible that Jessica has committed a wrong simply because authorities have a reasonable suspicion about her intentions. As this example with Jessica shows, there is a good case to be made that this offence is over-broad relative to the underlying moral desert of offenders, as it also encompasses actions that are either not culpable wrongs or at least not sufficiently so to merit such severe punishment (potentially up to fifteen years in prison).[13]

---

[13] It is little help that the Act allows one, as an affirmative defence, 'to prove that his possession of the article was not for a purpose connected with the commission, preparation or instigation of an act of terrorism', since individuals who blamelessly find themselves in circumstances the jury

One might thus see a tight connection between mala prohibita and over-broad offences – even if no one would take these two concepts to be co-extensive. Of course, the target conduct of preparing to commit an act of terrorism that section 57 of the Terrorism Act arguably sought to combat – perhaps on a proxy basis – is very plausibly malum in se, not malum prohibitum. Still, some might think that mala prohibita offences are problematic precisely insofar as they are over-broad and encompass conduct that is not wrongful or culpable (or at least not very much). Indeed, a similar concern will be the focus of our discussion of the wrongness constraint in a moment.

Nonetheless, we would resist this claim that mala prohibita are always or necessarily over-broad. As will become clear later (see Sections 1.4 and 4), there are interesting arguments purporting to show that many mala prohibita offences do, on closer inspection, involve significant forms of moral wrongness – albeit ones that depend on the state having good moral reasons for singling out new categories of conduct as crimes and the ways in which these reasons also serve to make the individual's non-compliance with such laws turn out to be morally wrongful. We will not ruin the surprise by spelling out the arguments of Section 4 now. But it remains a live possibility that on closer inspection some malum prohibitum offences might turn out to be wrongful and thus not actually over-broad at all. Still, it is plausible that the mala prohibita we really should be worrying about are those that display substantial overbreadth, as this would involve punishing the innocent or disproportionate punishment.

**Strict liability offences**. Strict liability offences allow one to be convicted without one being culpable or at fault in any way. More technically, these are crimes whose offence definition does not contain a mental state requirement (or *mens rea* – meaning 'guilty mind') as to one or more material elements of the offence definition, as the criminal law normally requires. In general, conduct is not a crime unless one had the right kind of mental state as to the consequences of or facts about what one was doing. The required mental state might be either an intention to produce those consequences or circumstances, knowledge they do or will obtain, awareness of a risk that they do or will obtain (recklessness) or at the very least being in circumstances that *should* have made one aware that these consequences or circumstances do or will obtain (negligence). Not requiring any such mental state as to certain material elements of the crime would mean that one could be convicted without being culpable or at fault in regard to

---

takes to be 'suspicious' may often have little concrete evidence available to prove their innocent intentions that would convince a jury. Furthermore, it is arguably unfair to the defendant to burden her with the task of exculpating herself in all such cases given the low bar that must be met for accusing her of this crime. See also text between notes 64 and 65.

those elements. Strict liability offences thus permit punishment even in the absence of a normative defect like fault, culpability or wrongness.[14] For example, if it is a strict liability offence to cause harm through transporting hazardous waste, then the statute would permit one to be convicted even if one took all possible precautions to ensure that it was transported safely – perhaps even far beyond industry standard and at great cost to oneself.

Criminal law scholars tend to be widely critical of strict liability offences because of the strong likelihood that they are over-broad (i.e. permit the punishment of those who are morally innocent).[15] To the extent they are supported, it tends to be on the basis of their perceived good consequences in terms of deterring the conduct at issue (i.e. on consequentialist rather than retributivist grounds – see Section 1.2; Hamdani 2007).

The important point here, however, is that there is no necessary connection between an offence being strict liability (either as to some or all its material elements) and being malum prohibitum. The state might well create mala prohibita offences that are strict liability for policy reasons such as the desire to make prosecutors' jobs easier. But the legislature need not adopt such heavy artillery in the laws they pass. Many mala prohibita do require a mental state element like knowledge or recklessness. For example, the licensing requirement Rhea violated at the beginning of this section requires that the malum prohibitum conduct at issue be done 'knowingly' (i.e. with awareness of the relevant facts). If one honestly believed the substance one was disposing of was pure water, not containing regulated forms of industrial waste, then one would not have committed the crime. Mala prohibita thus do not necessarily implicate the justificatory problems of strict liability crimes.[16]

Having now seen more clearly what mala prohibita are and what they are not, we can begin to appreciate that a legislature might have a potentially very broad range of reasons for creating mala prohibita offences. They might form central planks in a larger regulatory scheme aimed at combatting some particular problem – such as threats to public health, harms to our waterways or airways or harmful distortions of our financial markets. The legislature might find it beneficial to introduce a new malum prohibitum because it is a particularly useful proxy for some underlying harmful conduct that is especially hard to detect, or perhaps because it is useful as a way to enforce a licensing regime aimed at creating regulatory oversight over a new area of conduct (such as

---

[14] For more on the complex relation between wrongness and culpability (blameworthiness), see note 32.

[15] For a collection of sources criticising criminal strict liability, see Abbott and Sarch 2019: 352.

[16] Even if mala prohibita do not necessarily involve strict liability, it is a good question whether all strict liability offences are also mala prohibita.

trading in cryptocurrency). We will return to these justifications in more detail in Section 3. For now the point is just that mala prohibita have proliferated for a variety of reasons.

## 1.2 The Wrongness Constraint (and the View of the Criminal Law Underlying It)

This returns us to the original problem with mala prohibita: their apparent contravention of a fundamental principle of criminalisation, namely the requirement for the conduct criminalised to be morally wrongful. This wrongness constraint is a core part of a traditional approach to criminalisation, which we will now briefly outline.

### 1.2.1 Criminalisation in General

A theory of criminalisation is a set of principles and constraints that direct legislators in deciding whether to make a certain bit of conduct, C, a crime in order to ensure the laws they create are normatively justified. In a nutshell, a theory of criminalisation is likely to have the following structure:

> **Criminalisation Schema**. Making conduct, C, a crime, and thus subjecting those who perform it to a range of possible punishments, is justified if and only if
>
> (1)  the net benefit of criminalising C broadly construed – understood as the affirmative benefits (or reasons in favour) of such criminalisation minus its costs (or reasons against) – is at least as great as the net benefit of the available alternatives to criminalising C, including doing nothing (status quo) or merely imposing civil liability on C, and
> (2)  the act of criminalising C does not violate any of the applicable negative constraints (or limitations) on criminalisation.

Regarding (1), although the affirmative reasons for criminalisation are less pertinent to our main topic, a bit of background about them is important. While there is much debate about which affirmative benefits have priority, how they are related and whether some are reducible to others, the three most widely discussed[17] categories of affirmative reason for criminalisation are:

**Preventive benefits**. Criminalisation may help prevent harmful or wrongful conduct through mechanisms like deterrence or incapacitation. These are generally thought to be consequentialist benefits. Convicting and locking up

---

[17]  To see the broad influence of these categories of affirmative benefits, note that US federal law refers to the most widely acknowledged benefits, including the need to 'afford deterrence to criminal conduct', to 'protect the public from further crimes of the defendant', to 'provide the defendant with' rehabilitative treatment of various kinds, as well as to reflect 'the seriousness of the offense' which covers the wrongness of the act and the desert of the actor. 18 USC § 3553.

offenders can help reduce crime, for example, through incapacitation, preventing re-offending after release (specific deterrence) or deterring others from future similar crimes (general deterrence).[18]

**Retributive benefits.** Some think there is inherent value in giving wrongdoers the treatment they deserve in virtue of their wrongful (and culpable) conduct – and that this would be valuable even in the absence of any preventive benefits of punishment.[19]

**Expressive benefits.** There may be value in the state expressing official condemnation of certain especially egregious forms of misbehaviour through criminalising and subsequently punishing them. For example, this might be because of the value in the state recognising and reaffirming its commitment to protecting certain fundamental rights of citizens, reassuring all of us as potential victims, and in general influencing behavioural patterns in society through marking out certain forms of conduct as socially unacceptable.

We could debate which of these is fundamental. Some ask whether expressive benefits are a distinct category of reasons to punish or whether they simply reduce to consequentialist reasons because the ways in which expressing official condemnation can help reduce crime (Berman 2012: 148). Indeed, consequentialists may be especially likely to think harm reduction is the main justification for criminalisation and punishment and the other justifications matter only as a means to preventing harms.[20] Such views that take criminal law to have only one fundamental objective (to which all other justifications must be reducible) are **monistic**.

Arguably the more common position, though, is **pluralistic** about the aims and justifications of the criminal law.[21] Thus, the more common view is that in addition to seeking preventive benefits like reducing harm, a further aim of the criminal law is to do retributive justice (i.e. see to it that wrongdoers get their just deserts). Expressive aims may come on top of this again. Pluralists, in any

---

[18] Specific deterrence is the process whereby punishing a specific individual discourages that person from committing more crime in the future. General deterrence occurs when punishing an offender discourages *other* would-be offenders from committing crimes.

[19] See Moore 1997: 28–9.

[20] The law and economics literature tends to take this view (see e.g. Kaplow and Shavell 2002).
  Note also that retributivists might also seek to reduce the other reasons for criminalisation to their preferred category. Such a monistic retributivist might argue (1) that expressing official condemnation of wrongful conduct is part of what wrongdoers deserve for their misconduct (thus incorporating expressive benefits), and (2) that the kind of hard treatment that is owed to wrongdoers for their crimes must also be effective in reducing crime (so as to incorporate the deterrent justifications), because otherwise the state would show itself to be overly tolerant of (perhaps even complicit in) the serious wrongdoing that persists.

[21] As observed by Cahill (2011: 25), 'many have proposed a hybrid model of "limiting retributivism"' that 'combine[s]' consequentialism and retributivism, and that 'the ascendant view of punishment is more openly *pluralistic* about its purposes'. Berman (2012: 141–2) discusses the 'converg[ence] on a desert-constrained pluralism' about the justifications of punishment.

case, tend to be less concerned about which aims or justifications for criminal-isation and punishment are fundamental.

We take no stand on these issues here. The point is just that for criminalisation of a given type of conduct, C, to be warranted, the net benefits of doing so – *however these benefits are to be understood and whichever ones are to count* – must be at least as great as the net benefits of the available alternatives (including leaving the status quo in place rather than criminalising C).

In considering the net benefits of criminalising C, we must of course also take into account the *costs* this will have. Here 'costs' are likewise to be understood broadly (as indicated in Criminalisation Schema) – not just as financial costs, but as including all sorts of reasons against the proposed criminalisation. These include the harms that criminalising C will impose on those convicted and punished, as well as the harms it will impose on those investigated and accused of crimes under the new criminal law (as might count against very broad laws that allow law enforcement to intrude into private spheres of life). Similarly, we must also take into account the collateral consequences of punishment, such as the difficulty of reintegrating into society or harms caused to family or dependents of the incarcer-ated (Hoskins 2019). Assuming the benefits minus the costs (broadly understood) of the decision to criminalise C are at least as great as the similar net benefits of any available alternative to criminalising C, then it will be justified to criminalise C – *at least provided this does not violate any of the independent negative limits on criminalisation that apply.* Let us now consider some of those limits.

### 1.2.2 Negative Limits on Criminalisation

Theories of criminalisation also encompass negative limitations that can pre-vent otherwise justified legislative acts of criminalisation from being all things considered permitted. As Doug Husak noted, 'a comprehensive theory [of criminalisation] will include an exhaustive list of positive and negative reasons – reasons in favor of enacting criminal offences, and reasons against doing so' (Husak 2004: 213).

One much-discussed example is the Harm Principle, famously defended by J. S. Mill.[22] Applied to the criminal law, this is roughly the view that conduct may be properly deemed a crime and punished only if that conduct is harmful to the interests and rights of others besides the actor. What counts as harmful requires specification. Would merely causing offence count? What about

---

[22] In chapter 1 of *On Liberty*, Mill (2003 [1859]) writes, 'That principle is, that the sole end for which mankind are warranted, individually or collectively, in interfering with the liberty of action of any of their number, is self-protection. That the only purpose for which power can be rightfully exercised over any member of a civilised community, against his will, is to prevent harm to others.'

setbacks to another's interests in competitive contexts such as the marketplace? In any case, merely paternalistic punishments – whose only aim is to coerce individuals to act in ways that improve their well-being (on some conception or other of the good) – are very plausibly ruled out. (Sometimes the Harm Principle is offered as a positive reason for punishment, such as in Joel Feinberg's rendition,[23] but the details of where in the taxonomy of reasons for or against criminalisation a given principle most plausibly belongs need not concern us here.[24])

Other scholars include different limiting principles in their theories of criminalisation – including the wrongness constraint, which will be our main focus in what follows. Doug Husak, as a recent example, defended a theory of criminalisation containing four 'internal' principles that flow from the content of the criminal law (its general part). First, '[c]riminal liability may not be imposed unless statutes are designed to prohibit a nontrivial harm or evil' (Husak 2008: 66). Second, '[c]riminal liability may not be imposed unless the defendant's conduct is (in some sense) wrongful' (Husak 2008: 66). Third, '[p]unishment is justified only when and to the extent it is deserved'—i.e. should not be merely wrongful but also not disproportionate to the wrongdoer's desert (or culpability; Husak 2008: 82). Fourth, 'the burden of proof should be placed on those who favor criminal legislation' (Husak 2008: 100; Husak also defends several external constraints, which need not concern us here[25]). These examples are illustrative only. We cannot delve into the details of which negative constraints on criminalisation are most defensible, whether all deserve to be on the list or whether some can be reduced to others. Instead, let's look more closely at the constraint that is most directly in tension with mala prohibita – the wrongness constraint.

### 1.2.3 What Is the Wrongness Constraint, More Precisely?

The basic idea behind the wrongness constraint – that it is permissible to criminalise a bit of conduct only if it is morally wrong – stems from the view that there is a tight connection between morality and the criminal law, such

---

[23] Feinberg (1984: 30) writes, 'It is always a good reason in support of penal legislation that it would be effective in preventing (eliminating, reducing) harm to persons other than the actor and there is probably means that is equally effective at no greater cost to other values.'

[24] There also are more nuanced versions of the idea behind the harm principle. For example, John Gardner has suggested that in some cases of seriously wrongful conduct (e.g. rape), not criminalising it could cause harm – perhaps because failing to do so would send a devastating message to victims (Gardner: 2007: chapter 1).

[25] His two external principles are drawn from US constitutional analysis (akin to proportionality analysis in EU law). He thinks a justified criminal law both must serve a 'substantial' state interest and do so in a way that is no more extensive or burdensome than necessary (i.e. in a way that is suitably 'tailored' to the substantial state interest; Husak 2008: 130, chapter 3).

that it is the distinctive domain of the criminal law to proscribe and punish the most serious moral wrongs. This family of views goes by the name *legal moralism*, which Husak sketches as the view that 'we should recognize a presumption that the criminal law should ... be based on, conform to, or mirror critical morality' (Husak 2016: 34). At the very least, legal moralists think that this is the '[t]he default position [that applies] if insufficient reasons are marshaled in favor of the opposing point of view' (Husak 2016: 41).

If legal moralism is true, it provides motivation for the wrongness constraint (further arguments are considered later). If legal moralists are right that serious moral wrongs (perhaps just those of public concern) are the distinctive domain of the criminal law, then the criminal law would have no business proscribing and punishing conduct that is *not* morally wrong. Thus, it would be improper to criminalise conduct that is not seriously morally wrong, as the wrongness constraint requires.[26]

What is the notion of moral wrongness at work in the wrongness constraint? We follow Husak in taking this to be not *conventional morality* – captured in opinion surveys or anthropological work – but rather in what he calls *critical morality*, the content of which 'is ascertained through philosophical argument rather than a sociological poll' (Husak 2016: 33).

There are different ways to make precise the wrongness constraint (and different versions will become relevant in different sections of this Element[27]). Most important for us is whether the wrongness constraint is a **categorical constraint**, which cannot be overridden by countervailing reasons, or whether it merely is a **strong presumption**. Some theorists think (or are at least attracted to the view) that it would be unjustified to criminalise any conduct that is not morally wrong no matter the good consequences that could be obtained from criminalising such actions.[28] Other theorists (Husak 2016: 41; Cornford 2017: 634) think the wrongness constraint is merely presumptive and can be overridden by practical or consequentialist considerations (such as the need to make it easier for prosecutors to obtain convictions in some contexts).[29]

---

[26] Of course, the ideal embodied in legal moralism – that the criminal law should mirror morality – also pushes in a positive direction: it suggests that moral wrongness counts as a good, if defeasible, reason to criminalise. However, our focus is the wrongness constraint, which is the negative aspect of legal moralism that restricts us from criminalising morally innocent conduct. See Section 2 for more discussion of positive versus negative legal moralism.

[27] See e.g. note 30 and Section 5.

[28] Antony Duff indicates he is at least interested in seeing how far he can get in defending the categorical version of the constraint (Duff 2018: 61, 63).

[29] The wrongness constraint is perhaps easiest to understand with a deontological (non-consequentialist) view of morality in mind. Even on a consequentialist view, however, the question of which actions are morally wrong (in virtue of failing to maximise goodness) is still settled independently of which types of conduct the legislature should criminally prohibit.

For now, we take no stand on whether the presumptive or the categorical version of the wrongness constraint is most defensible, as our present aim is merely to lay out the options. For clarity, we will work with the categorical version for now until we have occasion to revisit the issue later. (Note also that some theorists introduce other versions of the wrongness constraint, though they are not important for present purposes.[30])

One might also wonder whether the wrongness constraint applies to whole categories of conduct – *act types* – or whether it rules out convicting and punishing particular instances of conduct by specific agents on particular occasions in specific circumstances – so-called *act tokens*. Because the criminal law's offence definitions – consisting of actus reus, mental state and circumstance elements – proscribe general act types, which permit a guilty verdict when unjustified and unexcused, it seems most natural to take the wrongness constraint to operate on whole act types. That is, the constraint would say that if a given act type is not a moral wrong, then it should not be criminalised. However, this masks a problem. Broad types of action, like lying or stealing or killing, of the sort proscribed by the criminal law, tend to be *morally unstable*. That is, the moral status of the particular tokens of such a type will vary depending on the morally relevant features of the specific case in question – the consequences, the agent's intentions, the justifications or excuses present, and so on. It is for this reason that philosophers, when engaged in first-order moral philosophy, tend to formulate theories as criteria for the moral wrongness (or permissibility) of act *tokens*.

---

On a consequentialist view, the wrongness requirement could still apply: it would permit criminalising only actions that are wrong on consequentialist grounds (because they do not maximise utility). It would then be a further question whether the wrongness constraint could be overridden because of the good consequences of doing so – and a committed consequentialist would presumably have no problem doing this. They likely would adopt only the presumptive version of the constraint – if indeed they adopt any version. See also note 33.

[30] For example, Duff (2018) defends the so-called strong wrongness constraint: 'we may legitimately criminalise a type of conduct only if it is wrongful independently of its criminalisation' (58). For Duff, criminalising act type X requires only that X it is wrong independently of the criminal law—either morally prohibited (mala in se) or prohibited by a justified non-criminal regulation. By contrast, Tadros (2012) defends a weak wrongness constraint: 'It is permissible to criminalize some conduct only if that conduct is wrong either independently of its being criminalised or as a result of its being criminalized' (158). The strong and weak wrongness constraints differ about whether the wrongness constraint is violated when X is a crime and purports to be wrongful only because there is a *criminal law* (not merely a non-criminal regulation) prohibiting it. The strong wrongness constraint says this violates the wrongness constraint: non-criminal wrongfulness is required for criminalisation. The weak wrongness constraint says the wrongness constraint is not violated: a criminal prohibition can provide the kind of wrongness that suffices to satisfy the wrongness constraint. Although an interesting issue, it does not affect the substance of our arguments so we set it aside here. See also note 48.

To avoid this difficulty, the most natural understanding of the wrongness constraint would be to say that, strictly speaking, it precludes an act type from being legitimately deemed a crime if it is not the case that *all act tokens* falling under the act type picked out by the offence definition are morally wrong when no affirmative defence is present. Thus, strictly speaking, if there is even a single act token falling within the offence definition that is not morally wrong (when no affirmative defence applies), then the wrongness constraint is violated.

It is also important to clarify that the wrongness constraint, as we understand it, operates on offence definitions subject to any justifications that may be applicable (though we mostly set aside excuses for present purposes). On the traditional picture,[31] offence definitions are supposed to correspond to pro tanto moral wrongs (i.e. actions that would be wrong simpliciter if there is no sufficient justification for the action). Thus, justifications – encoded in law as *justificatory defences* (like self-defence or the lesser-evils defence) – deny that some pro tanto wrongful conduct in the case at hand actually is a wrong simpliciter on the balance of reasons. By contrast, *excusatory defences* (like duress, provocation or involuntary intoxication) accept that a wrong simpliciter was committed (something properly deemed unlawful) but insist that the defendant was not *culpable* for it due to being subject to unusually challenging circumstances that we have sympathy for (such as grave threats to loved ones or having been drugged against one's will). Culpability, which focuses on how well or poorly an actor engaged with her reasons for action on the occasion in question, is a separate topic, which we largely set aside here. Instead, moral wrongness has to do with whether the act in question is decisively disfavoured by the applicable moral reasons bearing on how to act (whatever they may be) – that is, what one *ought not do* on the balance of (undefeated) moral reasons in the case at hand.[32]

---

[31] For a clear articulation of this picture, see Simester 2021: 17–29.

[32] What is the relation between the moral wrongness required by this constraint and the notion of culpability (or blameworthiness), which some legal moralists would take to generate a further constraint on criminalisation? The relation is complex if nothing else. On the one hand, consequentialist philosophers think the two notions come apart, as they think moral wrongness tracks the failure to maximise utility while culpability tracks something else, such as manifesting bad attitudes or disrespect for other persons in one's conduct (see e.g. Feldman 2006). Other philosophers hold that an action is morally wrong if and only if it is culpable (unless justified or excused; see Darwall 2006: 27; Mill 2004 [1861]: chapter 5, para. 14). We will assume the latter view here, as it helps simplify matters somewhat. If nothing else, it allows us not to have to say much about culpability (which on this view comes into play mainly in cases involving excuses – i.e. where there is an unjustified wrong that has reduced culpability because excused). Instead, this simplifying assumption allows us to focus the discussion primarily on wrongness.

Following this picture, we take the wrongness constraint to apply to criminal offence definitions subject to any justificatory defences that would deny the wrongness of the conduct. Thus, the wrongness constraint, to avoid criminalising innocent conduct, rules out two things: (1) declaring conduct that is not pro tanto morally wrong to be an offence (i.e. the basis for a conviction provided no justification or excuse exists) and (2) declaring conduct that might be pro tanto morally wrong but which has a moral justification to be a criminal offence unless the law includes some sort of carveout – most naturally, a justificatory defence – that ensures that actors who do the act with a moral justification actually are not convicted and punished for it.[33]

Putting all this together, we can precisely formulate our working version of the wrongness constraint as follows:

> **Wrongness Constraint (default version)**: It is permissible to criminalise a given type of conduct, T, *only if* all act tokens that meet the definition of T are morally wrongful (according to critical morality). More precisely, it is permissible to declare T to be a criminal offence *only if* all tokens that meet the legal definition of T either (1) are pro tanto wrongs that have no moral justification (i.e. are morally wrong simpliciter), or (2) if they are pro tanto wrongs that have a moral justification (i.e. are on balance permissible), then they fall within an affirmative legal defence that would prevent the agent of these act tokens from being convicted of T.

As an example of (1), suppose the legislature wants to make it a crime to use one's mobile phone for more than one hour per day. It is doubtful that tokens of this act type will be morally wrongful even when no moral justification applies. So this act type may not be declared an offence. As an example of prong (2), suppose the legislature wants to create a crime defined as the failure to recycle aluminium cans within one month of consuming their contents. Perhaps this conduct can be seen as morally wrong in the absence of any moral justification. So prong (1) poses no barrier. Nonetheless, some act tokens meeting the definition of this prohibited type might admit of a moral justification. For example, perhaps carrying out the recycling was unsafe under the circumstances (e.g. in a domestic violence context) or unduly burdensome (e.g. due to the demands of caring for a sick family member). Thus, if the legislature wants to proceed to create the offence with this sweeping definition (as opposed to

---

[33] It is perhaps easiest to understand the wrongness constraint if one assumes a deontological theory of what makes actions morally wrong. But the constraint is also intelligible on a consequentialist view. Whether an act token is wrong would be determined by asking whether it fails to maximise utility; it is a separate question which act types the legislature should criminalize. The wrongness constraint, on a consequentialist interpretation, would simply say: do not criminalize a type of conduct unless it is wrong by consequentialist lights. It is an open question whether the legislature's adherence to the wrongness constraint would maximise utility.

a narrower one), then it can permissibly do so only if it also ensures that there are sufficient affirmative defences to block a conviction for cases of act tokens that meet the definition but have a moral justification. This is what prong (2) is meant to ensure.

One might wonder if this construal of the wrongness constraint is too strict. Our formulation rules out any offence whose definition covers even one act token that is not on balance morally wrongful (at least if there is not also an affirmative defence to preclude a conviction for it). But real legislatures face epistemic limitations and cannot foresee every possible way in which a new offence might be committed. Moreover, they will have to work with vague and imprecise terms of a kind that are ineliminable in natural language. Thus, even with the best intentions of drafters, the very real possibility may remain of some act tokens that meet the offence definition but still would not be morally wrong even when lacking an affirmative defence. So is our formulation of the wrongness constraint not too strict?

It may be strict, and rarely fully satisfied in practice. But as a statement of the *ideal*, we still think it appropriate. When a legislature makes natural and unavoidable mistakes due to normal cognitive or epistemic limitations of human beings, and as a result ends up creating offences that cover some morally permissible actions (without creating sufficient affirmative defences to capture all of them), we think the violation of the wrongness constraint persists but may nonetheless be *excused*, which is to say not culpable. The violation of the constraint, however, puts pressure on the legislature to fix the overbreadth of the offence – either by narrowing the elements of the offence or by creating an affirmative defence of some sort. The greater the extent of the violation of the constraint – the more morally permissible act tokens that are inappropriately swept in under the offence definition once defences are also taken into account – the greater the injustice this entails and the greater the normative pressure on the legislature to amend the law to remove the violation.

### 1.2.4 What Motivates the Wrongness Constraint?

Why should we find the wrongness constraint attractive? As noted earlier, it might flow from a general picture of the criminal law as being particularly concerned with addressing serious moral wrongs. If one finds attractive this conception of the criminal law, insofar as this accounts for the particular gravity of the condemnation expressed by a criminal conviction (at least where the criminal law is just), as we do, then one will find some version of the wrongness constraint attractive.

Other arguments can further motivate the wrongness constraint. First, one might appeal to basic intuitions to directly support it. There arguably is a stable moral intuition that there is something seriously unjust about imposing punishment on those who have not done anything morally wrong. If the state criminalises and punishes wearing a sweater on Tuesdays merely in order to crack down on a disfavoured group of political rivals, then it might seem deeply unjust for individual sweater-wearers to be punished for such morally innocuous conduct. The wrongness constraint offers one natural explanation of why this seems beyond the pale.

This argument depends on one's sharing the right intuitions and so may not be the strongest basis for the wrongness constraint. A different kind of argument is suggested by Paul Robinson and John Darley's work (Robinson and Darley 1995, 2014). They contend that the content of the criminal law (its prohibitions and resulting punishments) must mirror common sense morality to a reasonably high degree or the criminal law will lose its perceived legitimacy in the minds of citizens. If that happens, they argue, it would no longer function as effectively as a mechanism for reducing crime. When the criminal law is no longer seen as a proportionate response to serious moral wrongdoing, and the legitimacy it is believed to have as a mechanism of justified social control is weakened, citizens will grow alienated and cynical and as a result are less inclined to respect the guidelines established by the criminal law. The result is to diminish an important tool the state has for reducing harm. If this is right, then it would mean there are good consequentialist reasons for the legislature not to criminalise some bit of conduct, C, unless C is at least widely believed to be morally wrong.

This argument is interesting as far as it goes, but worries remain. First, it can at best support a presumptive version of the wrongness constraint, not the categorical version. After all, in a scenario where greater consequentialist net benefits (e.g. in terms of harm reduction) can be had by not adhering to the wrongness constraint, then Robinson and Darley's reasoning would not stand in the way of departing from the wrongness constraint in particular cases.

Moreover, their argument does not ground a requirement that conduct be actually morally wrong according to *critical* morality (i.e. the morality that is best supported by philosophical and ethical theorising) but rather requires only that the conduct be morally wrong according to *conventional* morality. For example, imagine a society that believed interracial marriage to be immoral and criminalised it. One might want to combat such a law by marshalling the best empirical and ethical arguments to show that interracial marriage is fact is not morally wrong (i.e. according to *critical* morality), and then use the wrongness constraint to argue that this conduct is not justifiably criminalised. But this strategy would fail under Robinson and Darley's view because all their argument supports is a version of the wrongness constraint that rules out criminalising conduct that is not wrong according to *conventional* morality. But this would not rule out the criminalisation of interracial marriage in the present hypothetical.

Finally, there are deeper arguments based on core features of our criminal law, which support a version of the wrongness constraint that rules out criminalising conduct that is not actually morally wrong according to critical morality. This argument, which figures centrally in Section 2, appeals to the nature of the criminal law as a censuring institution. The idea is that in our criminal law system, a conviction is meant to carry a powerful message of condemnation. It communicates that the conduct is wrongful and sufficiently so to be publicly censured. The person convicted, moreover, is labelled a wrongdoer. However, these messages would be *false* if the conduct criminalised and for which one is punished is not actually morally wrong. Our system would thus be *dishonest* (or at least inaccurate) in communicating condemnation of people for pieces of conduct that actually are not morally wrongful. To prevent this, we must ensure that the conduct that gets criminalised, and which we can be convicted for, is morally wrong.

The key premise in this argument is that, in our system, to convict and punish someone for an action is to represent it as morally wrongful. This view has notable support (Duff 2014: 219–20; Simester and von Hirsch 2011: 19). Of course, if our system were *not* this way – perhaps we should change it so convictions do not send condemnatory messages of moral wrongness (a prospect that Section 3 explores) – then this argument for the wrongness constraint would crumble. Still, if this claim about our criminal law is correct, then we get a plausible argument for the wrongness constraint.

## 1.3 The *Mala Prohibita* Puzzle Revisited

If the wrongness constraint is true, how can mala prohibita be justified? What are we to say about actions prohibited by a malum prohibitum rule but the actor is justifiably certain that her act will not be harmful or bring about the evil the statute in question aims to prevent? The wrongness constraint seems not to allow such acts to be legitimately criminalised.

Rhea's case illustrates how thorny the problem is. Given her superior knowledge and skill, her conduct does not seem inherently dangerous, risky or otherwise irresponsible. As a result, one might wonder how it can it be legitimate to make her seemingly innocent conduct a crime. If she has not done anything that plausibly is morally wrong, then the wrongness constraint would preclude criminalising and punishing what she did. Cases like Rhea's are bound to come up regularly, and so the challenge is to understand why the many mala prohibita offences in modern legal systems are not broadly incompatible with the wrongness constraint.

Note that the task at hand is not to show why actors like Rhea have *self-interested* reasons to comply with mala prohibita laws. The fact that many actors will comply with mala prohibita laws for self-interested reasons is entirely unsurprising, and it does not address the question we are interested in: namely, whether the creation of malum prohibitum laws is itself a justified use of the legislative power, one that does not contravene fundamental principles of retributive justice on which our criminal law system is premised. Therefore, showing that Rhea has self-interested reasons to obtain the licence would not show her failure to do so to be morally wrong. Thus, in what follows, we largely set aside considerations of self-interest. For Rhea's crime to be an even clearer case of the puzzle we wish to confront, we can simply assume it is highly unlikely to be discovered. In this case, our question is whether she has any *morally* sufficient reason to obey the licensing requirement rather than just proceed to dispose of the waste in ways that are known to be perfectly safe and responsible? If not, how could her conduct be made a crime?

Notice that this is not an isolated case. Similar cases can arise across many different parts of the criminal law – from regulatory crimes relating to markets, the environment, and health and safety. (Indeed, a similar challenge arises for many over-inclusive or proxy crimes, where some non-wrongful conduct seems to fall within the offence definition.[34])

What would it take to resolve the puzzle of mala prohibita? There will always be some unwise or bad laws, the best efforts of law reformers notwithstanding. Accordingly, in seeking a solution to the malum prohibitum puzzle, the goal is not to show how every possible malum prohibitum offence – or every actual malum prohibitum offence in the legal system one is interested in – can be reconciled with the wrongness constraint. Rather, we are seeking a way to show that many, or perhaps a particularly important sub-set of, mala prohibita offences (such as those in service of a justified regulatory regime) can be rendered compatible with the wrongness constraint. That is, it would count as success if we can show that, *at least provided we are not dealing with obviously*

---

[34] For example, statutory rape can be seen as a proxy crime (see Duff 2018: 64; Cornford 2017: 639). Assume it is criminal for someone over 18 to have sex with someone under 16. This offence plausibly targets the underlying wrong of exploitative sex. However, there may be good reasons (like clarity and notice) to employ a bright-line rule with an unambiguous cut-off of 16 years to target this underlying wrong, even if it ends up making the offence over-broad. Now suppose an 18-year-old is in a committed, loving relationship with a very mature 15-year-old, and assume they have consensual, non-exploitative sex. Arguably, what the 18-year-old does is not morally wrong. If so, the offence would seem to violate the wrongness constraint.

*bad or unjustified laws, the mere fact that the offence is malum prohibitum in nature does not automatically mean that it is incompatible with the wrongness constraint.* This would be enough to count as a solution to the puzzle for our purposes. The result we are seeking a way to avoid, in other words, is the widespread incompatibility of mala prohibita offences, in general and as such, with the wrongness constraint.

## 1.4 Possible Solutions and Outline of the Element

In the remainder of this Element, we explore the different types of answers to the puzzle of mala prohibita. The two most natural responses can seem highly revisionary. The one explored in Section 2 would be to abandon the wrongness constraint and thereby change the nature and underlying aims of the criminal law. Alternatively, as discussed in Section 3, one might preserve a strong commitment to the wrongness constraint but reject mala prohibita offences. Both these strategies might seem to entail sweeping changes to the substance of the criminal law and how we understand it, though we consider the extent to which this is really the case.

In Sections 4 and 5, we explore more conciliatory responses to the problem. Section 4 explores philosophically sophisticated attempts to show that, despite first appearances, many core cases of mala prohibita offences (such as the case of Rhea) actually are morally wrongful and thus not really in tension with the wrongness constraint after all. In Section 5, we consider a further way to lessen the tension between mala prohibita and the wrongness constraint, although this involves weakening the wrongness constraint as well.

Through our discussion of the malum prohibitum puzzle, we hope to illuminate a number of fundamental principles of the criminal law and deep questions about our criminal law practices. We do not aim to conclusively answer these questions, though we indicate along the way what strategies appear most promising to explore further. In the end, we hope to show why the wrongness constraint matters to criminal law, why it can be tempting for the legislature to ignore it, and why society should be careful to craft criminal laws sparingly to avoid unjustified malum prohibitum laws. Finally, we hope this will also help illuminate the proper relationship between law and morality, and provide tools to evaluate whether specific malum prohibitum laws go too far to be legitimate.

## 2 Rejecting the Wrongness Constraint

One way to resolve the tension between mala prohibita and the wrongness constraint is to reject the constraint. This would mean that even if the conduct proscribed by a malum prohibitum rule is not morally wrongful independent from the law, this would not bar its criminalisation. The aim of this section is to examine more closely the arguments for and against the wrongness constraint, and assess how plausible it is to reject the wrongness constraint. This requires taking a closer look at what exactly we are doing when we criminalise and the nature and function of the criminal law.

## 2.1 Wrongness Constraint and the Nature and Function of the Criminal Law

One of the most ambitious legal moralist positions is Moore's. He argues that criminal law is a 'functional kind whose function is to attain retributive justice' (Moore 1997: 33) by punishing 'all and only those who are morally culpable in the doing of some morally wrongful action' (35). On his view, it is impermissible to criminalise conduct that is not morally wrongful. This is because punishing people for non-morally wrongful behaviour is to commit a retributive *in*justice.

One need not hold as ambitious a position as Moore's to endorse the wrongness constraint. In contrast, Duff (2018: 75) defends a 'modest legal moralism'. It is modest in at least two ways: First, unlike Moore who holds that there is reason to criminalise all moral wrongs in virtue of their wrongness, Duff argues that there is only reason to criminalise 'public wrongs' – that is, moral wrongs that properly concern the public (75–80).[35] Second, instead of Moore's metaphysically ambitious claim that criminal law is a functional kind, Duff argues that we should understand the criminal law as serving a distinctive and valuable role within a liberal democratic polity, namely to declare what constitutes public wrongs and to hold people to account for committing them (see Duff 2018: chapter 1). Duff's modest legal moralism also implies that it is impermissible to criminalise conduct that is not morally wrongful. This is because doing so subverts the criminal law by falsely declaring the non-morally wrongful conduct to be a public wrong and holding people to account for conduct that they ought not to be accountable for (55–70).

Against such legal moralist positions, Chiao (2018) argues for a more stripped down conception of the criminal law. On his 'public law conception', criminal law is a 'generically coercive rule-enforcing institution' whose aim is to 'stabilize ongoing social cooperation' understood paradigmatically as 'cooperation with legal norms established by public institutions' (45). Chiao thinks this aim is a basic function of the criminal law and has 'functional

---

[35] The thought is that not all moral wrongs are the business of and properly concern the public and the criminal law. Cheating on one's partner might be a non-public (private) wrong. Duff concedes that it is difficult to give a substantive, non-circular criterion for distinguishing public from private wrongs. For critical discussion, see Lee 2015; Edwards and Simester 2017.

priority' over other aims the criminal law just so happens to pursue, including retributive justice (46–51). Whenever any of these other aims conflict with this basic aim, then they should give way to the pursuit of the basic aim. More specifically, Chiao argues that the criminal law should be justified in the same way as public institutions are generally justified. He calls this 'a fully political standard of justification' (51–7). They should be 'subject to the constraints of political equality ... designed in such a way as to maximally promote effective access to central capability for all' (166), rather than to simply give people their moral deserts (168–72).[36] Chiao does not deny that the criminal law can sometimes be used to attain retributive justice or to declare and hold people accountable for public wrongs (51, 171, 174). It is just that it need not be used to achieve these legal moralist aims; and if it is used in those ways, it is justifiable only if this is consistent with and best helps to promote 'universal and effective access to central capability on terms acceptable to social and political equals' (167).

There is therefore no reason to endorse the wrongness constraint under Chiao's public law conception of criminal law. What ultimately matters to justifying criminalisation, on this view, is whether it is the best way to promote effective access to central capability for all under the constraints of political equality. Insofar as criminalising a certain bit of conduct is indeed the best means to achieving this, then it is justifiable even if the conduct is not morally wrongful. Indeed, for Chiao, one advantage of the public law conception is precisely that it can unproblematically account for mala prohibita because there is no wrongness constraint according to this view.

Limited space precludes a more detailed examination of Chiao's public law conception and his criticisms of legal moralism. What the remainder of this section will do instead is further explore the arguments for the wrongness constraint and ask what would be lost if we give it up. The view we end up with is an attractive position that lies between Chiao's public law conception and the more ambitious legal moralist positions.

## 2.2 An Argument for the Wrongness Constraint

### 2.2.1 Positive vs Negative Legal Moralism

To start with, we need to distinguish positive from negative legal moralism. According to the former, the moral wrongfulness of a bit of conduct is a reason for criminalising it. Negative legal moralism, by contrast, holds that we should

---

[36] 'A capability is central if it is required ... to live in that society as a peer, and [one] has effective access to it when she can exercise that capability without ... reasonable fear of interference' (Chiao 2018: 110).

not criminalise a certain bit of conduct unless it is morally wrongful. Thus, the wrongness constraint (as formulated in Section 1) is one more precise way to understand the commitments of negative legal moralism.[37] Positive legal moralism tells us when we have reasons to criminalise. Negative legal moralism does not tell us when we have reasons to criminalise, but only when we should not criminalise (Duff 2018: 55–8).

Legal moralists typically endorse both positive and negative legal moralism. This is the case for Moore and Duff: both hold that moral wrongfulness (or for Duff, public moral wrongfulness) is a positive reason for criminalisation and a necessary condition for justifiable criminalisation (Moore 1997: chapter 1; Duff 2018: chapter 2). Indeed, it is at least partly for this reason that their views are ambitious. Nevertheless, positive and negative legal moralism are separate positions. One can endorse either without endorsing the other. For example, one might hold that while moral wrongfulness is a reason for criminalisation, it is not necessary for justifiable criminalisation since it is justifiable to criminalise for other reasons as well. This is to hold a positive legal moralist position while denying negative legal moralism. Similarly, one might hold that it is never justified to criminalise conduct that is not morally wrongful (negative legal moralism), but deny that moral wrongfulness is a reason for criminalisation (positive legal moralism).

The point is that endorsing the wrongness constraint does not necessarily require an ambitious form of legal moralism. It simply involves defending a form of negative legal moralism (indeed, perhaps an even less restrictive version thereof than Duff's since we do not limit criminalisation to only 'public wrongs'). For clarity, we take no stand on positive legal moralism but remain ecumenical on the matter. The question then is what kind of unambitious or ecumenical argument can be offered for the wrongness constraint?

### 2.2.2 An Argument from Punishment

One popular argument draws on the connection between criminalisation and punishment. Criminalising conduct makes one at least liable to punishment if one commits it without a recognised justification or excuse.[38] If one thinks, like the (negative) retributivists (Duff 2003: 12), that it is undeserved and thus unjustifiable to *punish* someone for non-morally wrongful actions, then one might argue that it is also unjustifiable to *criminalise* such non-morally

---

[37] There are more restricted versions of negative legal moralism that are not the same as the wrongness constraint as we understand it. Duff's modest legal moralism is an example since it limits criminalisation to 'public wrongs'.

[38] Indeed, Husak (2008: 78) regards 'the identity of the criminal law with the susceptibility to state punishment as something approximating a conceptual truth'.

wrongful conduct, given the connection between criminalisation and punishment. This is to argue for the wrongness constraint on *criminalisation* from a claim about when punishment is unjustifiable.

We prefer not to rely on this argument because it is not ecumenical enough. It requires accepting the (negative) retributivist claim about the unjustifiability of punishing non-morally wrongful conduct.[39] Even if one finds that incontestable, one might contest that it is permissible to make someone liable for punishment only in cases where it is also permissible to actually punish her (Edwards 2017). One can also question the connection between criminal law and punishment. While some maintain a necessary and/or conceptual connection between criminal law and punishment,[40] it is at least possible to view this connection as a merely contingent one. One might see a difference between (1) the content of the criminal law (defining what crimes there are and the procedures for deciding when someone has committed them) and (2) punishment as a response to finding that someone has committed a crime. If the argument for the wrongness constraint relies on claims about (2), one might insist that it is properly speaking only a constraint on punishment and not automatically for criminalisation (or at most only when punishment so happens to be used as a response to crime).

One might also worry that the argument is unlikely to convince anyone who is not already sympathetic to the wrongness constraint. The premise of the argument – the (negative) retributivist claim that we must not punish without desert – is very similar in spirit to the conclusion the argument seeks to establish, namely the wrongness constraint on criminalisation. Therefore, if one is not already sympathetic to the wrongness constraint (and the close connection between criminal law and morality underlying it), then it's unlikely one will accept the main premise in the argument, namely that we should not punish without sufficient desert. The argument therefore may not move those who are not already inclined to accept the ideas underlying the wrongness constraint.

### 2.2.3 A Better Argument for the Wrongness Constraint

Accordingly, it is better to defend the wrongness constraint without relying on claims about punishment (see also Duff 2018: 15). Let us return therefore to the argument outlined in Section 1, based on what it means to criminalise conduct and the kind of messages communicated when we do so and then convict offenders for committing it. Our claim is that the criminal law does not speak

---

[39] One might reject this in favour of a 'fair opportunity to avoid' requirement instead. For discussion of this requirement, see Hart 2008: 18–24.

[40] Moore (1997: 33–5) does so in virtue of his functional kind claim about criminal law. See also Husak 2008.

in a morally neutral voice (Simester and von Hirsch 2011: 10–14). Despite the language often used in statutes (e.g. as when the Theft Act 1968 says, 'A person guilty of theft shall on conviction on indictment be liable to imprisonment for a term not exceeding seven years'), when we criminalise conduct, we are not simply declaring in a matter-of-fact way what will happen to those who are convicted of engaging in said conduct. Given how our criminal law system actually operates, we are also saying that it is *wrong* to engage in this conduct, that one ought not to. Indeed, it seems plausible to think that in many cases at least part of the explanation for why a certain bit of conduct is criminalised is that we (citizens or at least legislators) think that one ought not to engage in this conduct and that by criminalising it (not merely attaching civil penalties), we are publicly declaring this in an authoritative way to be the case.

There are good reasons for the criminal law to speak in such a moral voice. Addressing people in terms of what they ought or ought not do better respects them as autonomous agents capable of moral deliberations than simply announcing to them, 'if you do this, then you will be liable to suffer' (Simester and von Hirsch 2011: 10). The former seeks to engage with citizens' capacities for moral reasoning, while the latter seeks to largely bypass those capacities and attempts to secure their compliance by exploiting their natural aversion to pain and suffering.[41] If that is the case, then it is not just a brute fact that we understand the criminal law as speaking in such a voice. Rather, there are good reasons for the criminal law to do so; that a defensible criminal law is one that speaks to its subjects in such terms.

The same applies to criminal convictions. To convict someone of a crime is not simply to make a matter-of-fact statement that someone has been found to have engaged in certain conduct and therefore will now receive some treatment (e.g. imprisonment) according to some legal rules. Given that a crime is conduct authoritatively and publicly declared to be wrong (that one ought not do), convicting someone of a crime therefore implies *she* has done something wrong, that *she* has done something that she ought not. Indeed, the implication is that she has done the prohibited conduct *without justification or excuse*, since a conviction is not permitted if one has a justification or excuse (albeit only if it is legally recognised). Furthermore, if the crime includes *mens rea* elements (that are more than mere negligence), then a conviction also implies that those who are convicted did not simply end up doing what they ought not inadvertently or involuntarily. Rather, they had some awareness of what they were doing (e.g. risk harm to someone, take something owned by others, etc.). While this

---

[41] This does not mean that such threats cannot justifiably be used as 'prudential supplements' to the 'moral voice' (Simester and von Hirsch 2011: 14–16).

does not necessarily imply that they must also know what they were doing is a crime,[42] in cases where they do know (for whatever reason) that it is something they ought not do, then their conviction also implies that they have done so *culpably* without justification or excuse.[43] A conviction therefore marks someone out and shows her in a bad light. To convict someone is to say, inter alia, that she merits censure for committing something that is publicly declared a wrong without a justification or excuse. It is at least partly for this reason, we submit, that criminal convictions typically carry the kind of social stigma that they do.

More than casting the convicted in a bad light, a conviction involves *authoritatively judging* her so and *blaming* her for what she did. That is, it involves *censuring her* (understood as a kind of authoritative blame and rebuke) for her conduct. This does not simply involve (Zimmerman 2002: 555–6) entering a negative entry in the person's 'moral ledger' (quite literally in the case of criminal records), but also the expression of certain emotional and reactive attitudes that are characteristically warranted by wrongdoing. This is reflected in the use of language in statutes and the courts: one is not just convicted for an offence but is 'guilty' of it. As Simester (2021: 5) explains, 'A conviction makes a public, denunciatory statement about the defendant. It literally pronounces that she is guilty.' This is also reflected in the way courts describe and deliver their criminal judgements, which frequently involve ethical concepts and evaluatively laden language, especially when the case is particularly serious.[44] Indeed, some might even argue, pace Feinberg (1965), that '[t]he essence of punishment for moral delinquency lies in the criminal conviction itself ... It is the expression of the community's hatred, fear, or contempt for the convict which alone characterizes physical hardship as punishment' (Gardner 1953: 193).

If we are correct that our criminal law actually does, and moreover reasonably should, speak in a moral voice in condemning those who are convicted of criminal offences, then this generates an argument for the wrongness constraint. If there were no wrongness constraint and it was permissible to criminalise and convict people of non-wrongful conduct, then given that the criminal law properly speaks in a moral voice, it would mean that in convicting offenders who have done nothing that is truly wrong, the law would be speaking falsely. It would be declaring that the defendant committed a wrong that merits censure,

---

[42]  This is because ignorance of law is not typically a recognised defence.

[43]  This is not to say that negligent or inadvertent wrongdoing is not culpable. We leave this issue open here. If they are culpable, this would further strengthen our argument.

[44]  Admittedly this is more common at the sentencing stage. See e.g. United States vs Bernard L. Madoff, 09 CR 213, p.47: 5–13 (2009) (Chin, J.): 'Here, the message must be sent that Mr. Madoff's crimes were extraordinarily evil ... [I]n a society governed by rule of law, Mr. Madoff will get what he deserves, and will be punished according to his moral culpability.'

but if no moral wrong were committed, the criminal law's claim of wrongdoing expressed through the conviction would be false. Furthermore, if in criminalising conduct, the law marks it out as a public wrong that is not to be done (as Duff thinks), then the assertion of wrongdoing inherent in criminalisation would likewise be false if the conduct were not actually morally wrong.[45] In these ways, from the observation that the criminal law properly speaks in a moral voice, it follows that we should endorse the wrongness constraint to ensure that the criminal law does not speak falsely in its criminalisation of various forms of conduct and subsequent conviction of offenders.[46]

### 2.2.4 Revisiting the Public Law Conception and Legal Moralism

Given this argument for the wrongness constraint, we reject Chiao's public law conception and its characterisation of the criminal law as a 'generic coercive rule-enforcing institution' as being too thin. We do not deny that the criminal law is a kind of 'coercive rule-enforcing institution' but it is not simply a generic one. Rather, to the extent that it coerces and enforces rules, it does so in a particular way: by speaking in a moral voice. The criminal law authoritatively portrays crimes as wrongs and through convictions censures those found to have done them without justification or excuse. While this view of the criminal law is more substantive than Chiao's public law conception, it does not take us all the way to the kind of more ambitious (positive) legal moralist views like Moore's and Duff's. We do not claim that it is the *aim* of the criminal law to speak in a moral voice – we see it more as a feature of the criminal law. Nor do we think because it speaks in a moral voice, the aim of the criminal law must be a legal moralist one such as attaining retributive justice or holding wrongdoers accountable for their wrongdoings.[47] Our view is consistent with the criminal law having multiple aims and with there being a variety of different reasons for criminalisation, including but not limited to the positive legal moralist ones and – for example – harm prevention and the protection of individual rights. Our view is simply that whatever we aim to achieve that gives reason to criminalise,

---

[45] One might respond that it can still be justifiable for the criminal law to make such false claims because doing so can bring about weighty goods. We address this point in the next section.

[46] Note that an argument that is similar in spirit is also found by Simester (2021: 11): 'Given the social significance of the criminal conviction, and its role as a gateway to punishment, it is imperative that convictions, at least for serious offences, should be deserved. It is imperative that convictions should speak the truth.'

[47] It is worth clarifying that the claim here about the criminal law is an expressivist one: the criminal law speaks in a moral voice, and not that in so speaking, it is making *true* moral claims. Or to put it in another way, the criminal law makes claims of moral authority when it criminalises conduct and convicts offenders, but this does not imply it *does* have the moral authority it so claims. Section 4 will explore when and under what conditions the criminal law does have the moral authority in question.

the criminal law does so by speaking in a moral voice and this has normative implications for what can permissibly be criminalised.

What our view implies is therefore a form of negative legal moralism that is compatible with but not committed to positive legal moralism. The criminal law can be seen as a tool that serves a variety of purposes. Yet, it is a tool that has a particular feature (speaking in a moral voice) and this limits the range of things that it can be used against in the service of those purposes, whatever those purposes might be. As explained, this supports the wrongness constraint: unless it is respected, our criminalisation decisions and convictions will end up making false declarations and imposing erroneous censure.[48]

Unlike Moore, who sees criminal law as a functional kind whose essential purpose is to attain retributive justice, we do not take speaking in a moral voice to be a necessary feature of the criminal law. Rather, it is just a contingent feature. We can conceive of a criminal law that speaks not in a moral voice, but in a purely coercive one that is characteristic of a 'generic coercive rule-enforcing institution'. But we contend that this is not, or at least not the full picture of, how the criminal law operates in our society and how it is understood by citizens and officials in jurisdictions like ours. This is a claim about empirical social facts in systems like ours (the ones we are theorising about). We have not conclusively demonstrated it, but we think it is supported by the language used in statutes and by the courts, and in the way the criminal law operates procedurally, as illustrated in our argument about criminal convictions. Our argument for the wrongness constraint therefore is conditional on these empirical social facts being true and remaining true. Like other empirical social facts, this can change over time: we might come to see and understand the criminal law differently as it develops, or we might come to have good reasons for the criminal law to abandon speaking in a moral voice. If that were to happen (though it would not be without moral costs, given our argument about respecting people as autonomous agents), we accept that in that case our argument would not apply anymore and it would weaken the basis for the wrongness constraint. Finally, just like any other social facts that depend on peoples' views and perceptions, for our claims to be true in general does not require that everyone in society understands the criminal law in the ways we have sketched. After all, the claims that we are making here are grounded not simply in the fact that a majority of

---

[48] This does not imply that the only way to satisfy the wrongness constraint is to criminalise only conduct that are independently morally wrongful. This is because there may be ways for otherwise morally innocent conduct to be rendered morally wrongful by the law. Section 4 will explore this further and the extent to which this can help resolve the puzzle with mala prohibita (see also Section 2.2.3). Note also that we remain neutral on the strong versus weak wrongness constraint issue discussed earlier. See Duff (2018: 61–3) and note 30.

people and officials understand the criminal law in that way, but also in the language that the law uses and the structure of the criminal law. Indeed, we think there are good normative reasons for this feature of the criminal law that are grounded in respecting people as autonomous agents capable of moral deliberations.

## 2.3 Possible Criticisms

The remainder of this section will consider three criticisms of the wrongness constraint and the argument we have offered for it.

### 2.3.1 Presumptive Constraint and Mala Prohibita

One criticism against our argument is that it might fail to support a version of the wrongness constraint that is in tension with the existence of mala prohibita crimes. The idea is that the wrongness constraint we have argued for does in fact allow room for mala prohibita crimes. Sometimes it may be on balance justifiable for the state to make a false declaration about the wrongfulness of the conduct and falsely condemn a morally innocent wrongdoer due to the greater good secured by doing so. In other words, while there does seem to be a tension between mala prohibita and the wrongness constraint understood as an absolute constraint, it seems there is no (or much less) tension between them if the constraint is understood as a presumptive one. The worry is that the argument we offered for the wrongness constraint supports only a presumptive constraint (see Cornford 2017; and Duff 2018: 55–70, 235–7 for a response).

Even if all we could establish were a presumptive version of the wrongness constraint, however, it is not clear how much room it really makes for mala prohibita. Our view is that there is only little room for them since (1) there are reasons to think that the presumption is a rather strong one, and (2) the case for mala prohibita is seldom so weighty that without a particular mala prohibitum offence 'the heavens may fall'.

To see (1), recall that the kind of misrepresentation referred to in our argument for the wrongness constraint is not insignificant. Rather, it is a false representation about something that constitutes an authoritative standard for behaviour, which then forms a basis for criticising others and attracting social stigma. Marking someone out as culpably failing to do what one ought to do without justification or excuse calls into question her ability and trustworthiness to properly respond to reasons in her everyday life. The status of a culpable wrongdoer can also open the door to further negative (moral, social or legal) treatments that are warranted by her wrongdoing. The stakes are therefore quite high when it comes to the kind of false representation that underlies the argument for the wrongness constraint. Furthermore, this is a false representation made by the state and its officials (legislators and judges); and we are rightly more concerned about it, for reasons of transparency and legitimate use of power, when compared to false representations by a private individual. Given the content and actors involved in the false representations referred to in our argument for the wrongness constraint, there are good reasons to think the resulting presumption (even if only a presumption) should be a rather strong one.

On the other hand (and this relates to (2)), it seems the case for mala prohibita is seldom as weighty as typical cases in which core deontological constraints are justifiably outweighed. We do not deny that there can be some such cases. Perhaps the case for statutory rape offence is a good example. That is, perhaps the wrongness constraint can justifiably be outweighed by the need to have a bright-line age cut-off to be absolutely sure we are protecting children. However, it seems such cases may be few and far between. As we shall see in subsequent sections, the case for many mala prohibita do not really turn on, so to speak, matters of immediate life and death. Rather, the reasons for them typically relate to administrative efficiencies, the need to guide and coordinate behaviour, reducing the costs of enforcement, and making detection and prosecution easier.[49] Even if their end is ultimately about the prevention of serious harms, their value mainly lies in making it more efficient to do so rather than preventing otherwise unpreventable harms.[50] The choice is seldom just between enacting a malum prohibitum and doing nothing. Rather, it is often the case that we can also prevent the relevant harms through non-criminal regulations or with more targeted criminal offences that cohere with the wrongness constraint; it is just that they may not be as effective as enacting the malum prohibitum. The value of a malum prohibitum therefore lies, not with having it versus doing nothing and risking the ensuing harm, but with having it versus alternative means to prevent said harms. Our claim is not that mala prohibita often have little marginal benefit. We do think that many can bring about a non-trivial marginal benefit when compared to reasonable alternatives. Our contention is simply that this benefit seldom carries the level of weight that we tend to think is needed to outweigh a core deontological constraint on criminalisation like the wrongness constraint.

Therefore, even if the wrongness constraint is only presumptive, it would not ultimately be so much help in resolving the tension with mala prohibita. Still, for simplicity, we shall continue working with a categorical understanding of the wrongness constraint (though not an absolute one that is overriding in every

---

[49] See also Section 3.     [50] See also discussion in Section 4.1.2.

conceivable situation even when 'the heavens may fall'). A categorical under-standing better captures the weight and importance of the considerations in favour of the wrongness constraint that were discussed in relation to (1) – namely, that the state and its officials have a duty (not merely reasons) to avoid making a false declaration about the wrongfulness of an action and falsely condemning offenders as culpable wrongdoers when they are not.

There is also a methodological advantage to starting with a categorical understanding of the wrongness constraint. It forces us to look harder for ways to accommodate mala prohibita within the constraint before concluding that they can only be accommodated by way of a (perhaps regrettable) lesser-evils (or consequentialist-style) justification. Starting with a presumptive under-standing of the constraint, on the other hand, would make it easier to avoid the hard work of working out how mala prohibita can be accommodated within the wrongness constraint, strictly construed.

### 2.3.2 Over-generalising the Fact that the Criminal Law Speaks in a Moral Voice

The second criticism goes to the heart of our argument for the wrongness constraint. According to this criticism, the criminal law does speak in a moral voice but only for those that are independently morally wrongful (mala in se). It is because the criminalised conduct is independently morally wrongful that criminalising it amounts to declaring that it is a wrong and convictions thereof censure. But if so, the criticism goes, then we have over-generalised our claim about the criminal law speaking in a moral voice. It does not actually always speak in a moral voice. It depends on whether what is being criminalised is something that is independently morally wrongful. If the criminal law does not speak in a moral voice across the aboard, according to this objection, our observations do not support an across-the-board wrongness constraint for all criminalisation.

Perhaps historically one main reason why the criminal law came to speak in a moral voice is that early criminal law focused primarily on independent moral wrongs like murder, assault and fraud. Still, we suggest that given the criminal law speaks in a moral voice as to such paradigmatic crimes, it has come to be widely understood as speaking in such a moral voice for any conduct that is deemed a crime. That is, by being declared a crime, a piece of conduct is declared to share something important with core mala in se like murder, assault and fraud: they are things that are authoritatively declared to be wrongs that one ought not do and being convicted thereof conveys blame for one's conduct. A telling bit of evidence for this interpretation is that the criminal law in its everyday operation does not actually draw a hard and fast line between paradigmatic crimes considered to be independent moral wrongs and other crimes that are not. Theorists may distinguish between mala in se and mala prohibita, but the criminal law does not categorically treat the former in a different way than the latter.

Thus, even if *in principle* the criminal law could have spoken in a moral voice for some crimes but not others, it seems unlikely that this is how the system is actually perceived, given that the criminal law does not in its official capacity and everyday operations draw such a distinction but instead treats all criminal offences equally as crimes and subjects them to the same procedures. We suggest that the most natural interpretation of the criminal law therefore is that it is understood to be speaking in the same moral voice for all crimes. Accordingly, we think it remains plausible that the wrongness constraint should apply broadly to all instances of criminalisation.

### 2.3.3 Is the Wrongness Constraint Redundant?

The third criticism is that the wrongness constraint is redundant. As we have presented it, the constraint does not require that conduct, to be criminalised, must be mala in se; it simply must be wrongful – regardless of the reason why (including the operation of law). However, Chiao (2018: 172) objects that if the wrongness constraint 'is interpreted more generously to include conduct that is wrongful only because prohibited by just public institutions', then 'it appears trivial [and] simply restate[s] the claim that the offence-creating law is just, except in the language of right and wrong'.

This objection is not persuasive. As we discuss further in Section 4, mala prohibita are not rendered morally wrongful by the law (if and when they are) simply because the legal prohibition of the action, A, is justified. Additional conditions also need to be satisfied to make it morally wrongful for an individual to perform a particular instance of A'ing. Plausibly, even when it is justifiable for the legislature to pass a law prohibiting A'ing (whether criminal or merely a regulation), there could still be instances where it is not morally wrong for specific individuals to do an act of A'ing. These are not only cases involving a recognised legal justification, but perhaps also factors the law will be more reluctant to recognise, such as claims of special expertise or idiosyncratic circumstances of the particular actor.[51] In such cases, even if the legislature had good reasons to prohibit A'ing and enforce it through sanctions, something further is needed to explain why it would be wrongful for the individual to do A (that is, why the legislature's reasons for proscribing A should bear on whether the

---

[51] The case of Rhea from Section 1 is an example.

individual ought not to A). This fact – that it is morally wrong for the individual to do A – in turn, would be necessary to satisfy the wrongness constraint and thereby render it permissible to make it a crime to commit acts of A'ing.

There are two different questions in play here. First, we might ask whether the legislature has sufficiently good reason to prohibit A. By contrast, we might ask whether the individual's performance of A (the malum prohibitum offence in question) is *rendered morally wrongful by the law* despite it not being so independently of law. The former assesses the *justifiability* of the decision to legally prohibit A and depends on the legislature's reasons for or against doing so. The latter is about the law's (or the state's) ability to alter the moral duties of individual actors or create new ones.[52] This concerns what political philosophers call the *authority* of the law's directives to do or refrain from this or that action. A legal directive issued by the state is authoritative when it is a successful exercise of the state's power to impose or create morally binding rules and duties on the citizens it applies to.[53]

Notice how the justifiability of prohibiting A can come apart from its being morally wrong for the individual to A. They are not simply two sides of the same coin. If it is *justifiable* for the state to legally prohibit A, this implies that it does not (all things considered) have a duty against prohibiting it and enforcing the prohibition through appropriate sanctions. The state does no wrong in doing so and we, as citizens, have no right against the state doing so. This, however, does not by itself imply that individuals do wrong in failing to comply with the legal prohibition against A. It does not imply that we are morally criticisable if we fail to comply with it or that we are not at liberty to refuse to comply. On the other hand, if the state, in prohibiting A, were to *successfully* exercise its authoritative power to make it morally wrongful for one to perform A, then this implies we now do not have the liberty to do A. The successful exercise of authority implies that it is wrong for us to do A and that we are morally criticisable for doing so.

Accordingly, in cases where doing A is not independently wrongful, what is needed to satisfy the wrongness constraint would be the law's authority to render doing A wrongful. The justifiability of the law's prohibition of A alone is insufficient. After all, we cannot assume that the legislature's high-level

---

[52] This can be an instance of 'robust reason-giving' or an instance of 'merely triggering reason-giving'. We do not need to take a stand on this here. For a discussion of the difference, see Enoch 2014.

[53] The terminology used in the literature can be confusing. Simmons (2001: chapter 7) distinguishes 'justification' from 'legitimacy' in a way that tracks our distinction here. But Wellman distinguishes between 'political legitimacy' which 'concerns the state's right to coerce its constituents' and 'political obligation' which 'involves a citizen's duty to obey the laws of her state' (741).

reasons for proscribing A will automatically be reasons affecting what the individual ought to do (at least we cannot assume this without more explanation of why). We accept that the justifiability of passing a law that prohibits A might very well be a *necessary condition* for this prohibition to also be authoritative (i.e. for it to be wrongful for us as individual citizens to do A). However, the former does not straightforwardly imply the latter, at least not unless certain additional conditions are also satisfied.

In Section 4, we will discuss some candidate accounts of when and why it is not only justifiable to declare A'ing to be a malum prohibitum crime, but the legal prohibition of A'ing is also authoritative – that is, makes it wrongful (when it is) for individuals (even those with special skills or expertise) to do A. These considerations, we will see, could range from a moral duty to uphold just institutions to considerations of fair play to the civic responsibilities that citizens owe one another. Details aside, the key point here is that some additional considerations like these are needed to explain why it is morally wrongful for individuals to perform an act of A'ing besides the mere fact that it was justified of the legislature (perhaps on consequentialist grounds) to prohibit A'ing. As a result, the wrongness constraint – because some such additional considerations must be present to ensure moral wrongfulness – is not redundant. It does not (as Chiao alleges) merely restate in moral terms the requirement that there are good reasons supporting the legislature's decision to prohibit A'ing. While such justifiability might very well be a *necessary* condition for mala prohibita to be consistent with the wrongness constraint, this is not by itself sufficient.

## 2.4 Conclusion

In this section we argued for the wrongness constraint from the premise that our criminal law speaks in a moral voice and that it is crucial for the representations the law makes especially in convictions not to be false. This helps to show what would be lost if we were to abandon the wrongness constraint and begin to criminalise even more freely than we already do. In particular, it would further dilute the claims of wrongness and censurability that we argued the criminal law properly makes in a moral voice. Insofar as we continue to expect the criminal law to speak with a moral voice, then failing to respect the wrongness constraint in criminalisation would produce more false declarations by the criminal law. This, in turn, could weaken the trust and perceived legitimacy citizens attach to the criminal law.[54] This, as Robinson has argued, would threaten to erode the efficacy of the criminal law as a guide to appropriate behaviour that citizens are

---

[54] This, of course, assumes that citizens' moral views (i.e. conventional morality) broadly reflect critical morality, which is what determines the content of the wrongness constraint.

disposed to voluntarily comply with.[55] Accordingly, dispensing with the wrongness constraint could weaken the criminal law's ability to express the moral messages we plausibly want it to and thereby serve important functions (including voluntary compliance and addressing citizens as autonomous moral reasoners) that we want it to promote. This is not to say it would be impossible to make do without a criminal law that speaks in a moral voice, but it is important to be cognisant of the potential costs that this could carry.

Accordingly, if mala prohibita conflict in substantial and pervasive ways with the wrongness constraint, then perhaps it is the mala prohibita themselves that should yield. We explore this strategy in the next section.

## 3 Reject *Mala Prohibita*?

In the previous section we considered what it would mean for the criminal law to give up its commitment to the wrongness constraint. Since we saw this had drawbacks, we should next explore the opposite response to the mala prohibita puzzle: remaining committed to the wrongness constraint but rejecting mala prohibita insofar as they conflict with this constraint.

As suggested in the previous section, our criminal law system appears to contain a deep-seated commitment to the legal moralist ideal of the criminal law mirroring morality, particularly as expressed in the wrongness constraint. If so, then it may seem that many malum prohibitum crimes in fact are improperly criminalised. This suggests we must eliminate or reduce the prevalence of mala prohibita offences in our system, as well as refrain from adding more. What would this mean for the legal system?

The natural worry about this strategy is that eliminating mala prohibita that conflict with the wrongness constraint might have radical implications for the law – particularly regulatory frameworks in which mala prohibita figure centrally. Thus, the required revisions to the law might prove be too costly to be acceptable. The costs of eliminating mala prohibita that conflict with the wrongness constraint depend on several factors: (1) what benefits would be lost from their elimination and (2) how often mala prohibita unavoidably conflict with the wrongness constraint.

---

[55] Robinson (1996: 212–13) states, 'The real power to gain compliance lies not in the threat of official sanction, but in the power of ... internalized norms. ... Criminal law ... plays a central role in creating and maintaining the consensus necessary for norms ... If it earns a reputation as a reliable statement of what the community perceives as condemnable and not condemnable, people are more likely to defer to its commands as morally authoritative ... The extent of the criminal law's powers [in this respect] is directly proportional to the criminal law's moral credibility.' See also Husak 2020.

This section examines both factors in more detail. Section 3.1 considers the benefits of mala prohibita and what would be lost if we eliminated them or dramatically reduced their frequency. Section 3.2 investigates precisely what would be ruled out by rigorously applying the wrongness constraint. This helps us see how widespread the conflict between mala prohibita and the wrongness constraint is likely to be, and thus how radical it would be to pursue the strategy of this section.

Note that this section proceeds on the assumption that there *is* robust tension between mala prohibita offences generally and the wrongness constraint. In the next section, we will scrutinise this assumption by considering arguments that, despite first appearances, much malum prohibitum conduct is actually morally wrongful. This section, by contrast, brackets such arguments and takes the first appearance at face value in assuming that typical mala prohibita do conflict with the wrongness constraint. Thus, this section investigates how radical it would be to side with the wrongness constraint in the face of such a conflict with mala prohibita.

## 3.1 What Would We Lose in Rejecting *Mala Prohibita*?

Eliminating or seriously curtailing the use of mala prohibita to better respect the wrongness constraint may not be top of the criminal law reform agenda in many jurisdictions. We do not see much public ire about criminal sanctions being applied to malum prohibitum conduct – such as the sometimes surprising anti-money-laundering rules (like the requirement to report large cash transactions), or that one must register securities to be allowed to sell them, or that one must obtain licences to legally carry out a range of potentially dangerous activities that nonetheless have social value (Green 1997). Perhaps this has to do with the low regard in which traditional limits of the criminal law, such as the wrongness constraint, are held in public discourse. Perhaps it stems from the force of arguments like those explored in the next section purporting to show that malum prohibitum conduct can indeed sometimes be morally wrongful, despite first appearances. Moreover, the lack of pressure to reform our reliance on mala prohibita offences likely also has to do with the immediate necessity of confronting serious systemic challenges in anglophone jurisdictions, such as ending mass incarceration in the United States and adequately funding the criminal justice system in England and Wales.

However, equally important in explaining why mala prohibita are not a target of urgent law reform efforts is surely also the widespread sense of the *good* that can be accomplished through mala prohibita particularly in regulatory contexts – notwithstanding any justice concerns stemming from their possible lack of moral wrongness. Insofar as a malum prohibitum offence is part of the legislature's attempt to regulate a given industry or activity in pursuit of justified state aims (like public health, worker safety, environmental protection, efficient and trustworthy markets), this offence might be thought to enjoy normative support as a means to these goals.

### 3.1.1 Benefits of Mala Prohibita

What, then, are the typical benefits of mala prohibita offences, which we would stand to lose without such offences?[56]

**Clarity (guiding action and protecting privacy).** If crafted appropriately, mala prohibita can realise the advantages of clear bright-line rules. This means making use of easy-to-discern, objectively verifiable features or requirements. An example might be the requirement to report cash transactions over $10,000 to the authorities. Making the failure to do so a crime enables oversight over transactions with a higher-than-normal likelihood of facilitating money laundering. The cut-off of $10,000 may seem arbitrary. Would a $9,800 cash transaction not carry a comparable probability of money laundering? But there are tangible benefits to such a simple, verifiable cut-off. First, it provides clearer guidance to citizens about exactly what conduct is required (or forbidden). Had the rule said, for example, that cash transactions must be reported to the tax authorities when 'reasonably necessary to avoid any undue risk of facilitating money laundering', this might seem more like a malum in se offence, but it would also be vastly more ambiguous and that generates uncertainty about what conduct is off limits. Therefore, mala prohibita can function as bright-line rules, thus making it easier for regulated parties to know how to behave. Furthermore, by reducing ambiguities, bright-line rules remove the need for individual interpretation, which otherwise can make actors more likely to make the wrong decision – or more worryingly, might be used in self-serving ways to justify socially undesirable conduct.

Clarity in the law also can protect privacy. Most would wish to avoid being investigated by law enforcement. If, thanks to the clarity of a bright-line rule, citizens can be more confident they are not violating the law, they can likewise be more confident they will not be investigated by law enforcement (at least all else equal in a just legal system). By contrast, if the law employs more ambiguous evaluative concepts, this increases the degree to which citizens are left open to the risk and anxiety of being investigated.

---

[56] These benefits are not unique to mala prohibita; they may also be characteristic of other types of offence as well, such as proxy crimes.

**Detection benefits for law enforcement**. By allowing the legislature to define the offence as it sees fit – rather than needing to fit the contours of an existing malum in se behaviour which may involve ambiguous evaluative concepts (like 'unreasonable', 'necessary' or 'dishonest') – mala prohibita offences allow the use of elements that are easier to observe. This means the offence can be defined to make it easier for law enforcement to detect when the conduct has occurred. It can of course still be difficult for the police to determine how much cash changed hands in a covert money-laundering transaction. But it is much easier to discern whether more than $10,000 changed hands without a report being submitted than if the offence is defined, for example, as failing to report a cash transaction when doing so was *reasonably necessary* to avoid undue money laundering risks. Were it the latter, not only would law enforcement have to determine the amount of cash that changed hands, but also whether in the circumstances a report should have been filed due to an unreasonable money laundering risk. Similarly, the difficulty of deciding when there is reasonable suspicion (or probable cause) that the offence was committed – to justify more intrusive forms of investigation or arrest – would likewise go up significantly. Legislatures can eliminate substantial difficulties for law enforcement by passing mala prohibita offences with easier to discern (albeit sometimes more arbitrary) elements – instead of more ambiguous (if also more normatively accurate) concepts. Such benefits would be largely lost if legislatures could not make use of mala prohibita.

**Ease of proof and prosecution**. Mala prohibita can confer similar benefits on prosecutors. Mala prohibita that are clearly articulated in terms of objectively verifiable qualities tend to be easier for prosecutors to prove in court. With the malum prohibitum of failing to submit such a report for a cash transaction over $10,000, all the prosecution must prove is that the amount of the transaction exceeded $10,000 (and the defendant knew it) but no report was filed. By contrast, if the offence were to fail to submit a report when reasonably necessary to avoid undue risk of facilitating money laundering – a description that better picks out the harms or wrongs to be prevented – the prosecutor's job would be much more difficult. Besides proving the amount of the transaction and absence of a report, they would also have to bring in expert witnesses to testify about what sorts of transactions carry substantial risks of facilitating money laundering and explain why filing a report in this instance was reasonably necessary to avoid such risks. Accordingly, the proof needed to establish beyond a reasonable doubt that the offence was actually committed goes up considerably. Mala prohibita can therefore increase the efficiency of prosecutions, which some might argue also carries deterrence benefits in certain circumstances.

**Regulatory benefits**: In addition, mala prohibita also derive support from the regulatory schemes in which they figure. If mala prohibita are a means to obtaining the benefits of a specific regulatory scheme, then to the extent these benefits cannot be obtained in other reasonable ways without mala prohibita, then the benefits of this regulatory scheme would also be set back if mala prohibita must go.

Modern states need to regulate conduct in a wide array of activities and contexts. In industrialised societies with a complex market economy, a range of regulations are needed to protect citizens from harm: from protecting the health and safety of factory workers to protecting citizens from toxic emissions from industrial activity, from protecting consumers from unsafe products or dishonest advertisements to protecting market participants from predatory sellers or sophisticated players who unfairly take advantage of those with less expertise. At times, strong incentives, including criminal sanctions, may be needed to get self-interested actors to abstain from profitable but harmful activities. Given the benefits described in this section (including ease of detection and prosecution), mala prohibita can be a helpful tool in service of these aims. Therefore, where mala prohibita offences serve as integral parts of a regulatory scheme that provides protections for citizens, such regulatory aims might be impeded if the legislature could not legitimately use mala prohibita offences as a tool due to their conflict with the wrongness constraint.

### 3.1.2 Alternatives to Mala Prohibita

This raises a central question: how necessary is a particular malum prohibitum to the attainment of the general regulatory goals of the scheme that it figures in? Can the scheme's benefits, and the promotion of the underlying regulatory goals, be obtained without using mala prohibita? If so, we would not feel the loss of mala prohibita offences so heavily. The extent to which a given malum prohibitum rule is necessary for the efficacy of the regulatory framework it is a part of depends on several factors, including (1) the necessity of this offence to the regulatory scheme and (2) how well the scheme can function without this offence in place, which depends on what the feasible alternatives to using mala prohibita offences are.

It is difficult to say anything general about (1). It will depend on the details of the regulatory framework and the offence. But we can say something more generally about (2). Considering alternatives to mala prohibita helps give a better sense of how much strictly applying the wrongness constraint would frustrate particular regulatory schemes or whether such schemes can reasonably reduce their reliance on mala prohibita.

One natural alternative is to use mala in se offences instead. However, this would likely carry the drawbacks seen in the previous sub-section. Insofar as defining the mala in se in question requires using more nuanced or multi-faceted normative concepts like 'unreasonable', 'undue', 'necessary', 'dishonestly', and so on, the offence will be likely to provide less clear guidance, be more easily gameable, as well as be more difficult to detect and prosecute.

Therefore, the more important alternative to mala prohibita to consider is the use of non-criminal approaches. For example, one might find it far less problematic to impose tort liability (also called civil liability) on conduct that would amount to a malum prohibitum offence if criminalised. Tort liability, roughly put, merely aims to negate or correct unjustly imposed harms or losses (e.g. through paying compensation or other forms of redress[57]) as well perhaps as seeking to encourage efficient behaviour along the way.[58] As a result, many theorists would not think there is a comparably strong wrongness constraint on deeming actions to be tortious as there is on making conduct a criminal offence.[59] Thus, tort law may seem less problematic as a mechanism for encouraging compliance with appropriate regulatory schemes than mala prohibita offences within the criminal law.

Indeed, government agencies are sometimes empowered to regulate entities or individuals by bringing private actions in court in an analogous way as prosecutors bring criminal charges. The Securities and Exchange Commission's enforcement of securities laws and regulations is a nice example, as the Commission brings civil enforcement actions for violating securities laws while the Department of Justice brings analogous actions to enforce the criminal aspects of these laws. Often the same conduct can be targeted both through filing civil and criminal actions in court, and in the case of securities fraud similar liability standards are sometimes used (Buell 2011: 548–61).[60] So there are precedents for relying on civil liability in areas where the criminal law needs to be supplemented.

---

[57] See Coleman 1992: 198; Hershovitz 2011.

[58] This primacy of encouraging efficient behaviour is endorsed by economic theories of law (Kaplow and Shavell 2002).

[59] We are not claiming there is no tort analogue to the wrongness constraint. Several recent influential accounts of tort identify an important connection between torts and wrongs (Goldberg and Zipursky 2020; Gardner 2020; Hershovitz 2017). Nonetheless, the content of wrongs for tort purposes may well be different than for criminal law, meaning the two areas might differ in the actions they view as wrongful. Tort law tends to be more concerned with notions of responsibility (causal responsibility or agential involvement) than *culpability* – i.e. failures of practical reasoning manifesting disrespect for others – which is the more specific concern of criminal law. Clarifying the relation between tort and criminal law, however, is beyond the scope of this Element.

[60] The available remedies may differ, though tort law can also include some retributive or condemnatory element as well in the form of punitive damages.

In addition to making use of such private law actions (whether initiated by individuals or agencies), another alternative to criminal mala prohibita would be for government agencies or public bodies to directly regulate the relevant conduct ex ante – via administrative orders, monitoring, reporting requirements and non-criminal fines or penalties of various kinds. For example, the conduct of healthcare professionals might be directly regulated through a licensing body, where misconduct can result in the loss of one's licence to practice or other remedial actions.[61] Such direct regulation is another alternative (or supplement) to criminalising different forms of failure or misconduct within the relevant profession or activity. (There may be more radical alternatives as well involving creating new types of legal institution, but we set those aside as they will be far more controversial.[62])

Given such alternatives to the use of mala prohibita to support a given regulatory framework, there may be quite a few cases in which the mala prohibita crimes within the regulatory scheme could be excised without dramatically compromising the efficacy of that scheme. Of course, we would lose the condemnatory force that a criminal conviction carries, and the powerful message sent about the limits of what behaviour society will tolerate, which is conveyed by criminalisation and punishment. But perhaps the loss in terms of promoting valuable regulatory goals would not be unmanageably high as a result of cutting out mala prohibita crimes – at least not always. This must be a case-by-case determination. But it is not clear the regulatory world would come crashing down if we were to rigorously apply the wrongness constraint and back off from using mala prohibita crimes in service of regulatory goals. It might entail some loss of efficiency, but the extent of this cost remains to be seen.

## 3.2 How Widespread Is the Conflict Between *Mala Prohibita* and the Wrongness Constraint?

Thus far, we have asked what benefits might be lost if we eliminated or reduced our use of mala prohibita in regulatory contexts. We considered some available alternatives and we had reason to wonder if perhaps the costs might not be unmanageably high. All this was to help assess how radical it would be to rigorously apply the wrongness constraint.

---

[61] In the United Kingdom, for example, healthcare professionals are primarily regulated by the Health & Care Professionals Council (Health Act 1999 s. 60), which can apply non-criminal penalties like restricting or revoking a licence to work in the affected professions. Healthcare professionals remain subject to criminal law, of course.

[62] For example, the state might establish a system of non-stigmatic administrative violations, where mere fines are imposed rather than full-fledged convictions and punishments that express condemnation. The wrongness constraint would not apply to such a system. See Walen 2020: 434; for critical discussion, see The Law Commission 2010: paras. 3.28–3.37.

But there is a logically prior question to consider. To assess how radical strictly applying the wrongness constraint would be, we must also ask how widespread the conflict is between mala prohibita and the constraint. When would the wrongness constraint rule out an entire offence and how frequently would this occur? To get a sense of how widespread the conflict between mala prohibita and the wrongness constraint is, we would have to estimate not only how many mala prohibita offences there are in our body of criminal law, but also what proportion of these would be ruled out by the wrongness constraint.

To answer either question even approximately would take serious empirical work. Given practical limitations, we must leave such empirical inquiry to others. However, we can still help illuminate the matter by addressing the conceptual question of what it would take for a given malum prohibitum offence to be ruled out by the wrongness constraint and what options this would leave the legislature.

As seen in Section 1, the wrongness constraint operates at the level of act types. It assesses the legitimacy of a candidate offence definition subject to any affirmative defences (justifications or excuses) that may apply. Strictly applied, the wrongness constraint would preclude a given offence if it is not the case that *all act tokens* picked out by the offence definition are moral wrongs when no relevant affirmative defence is present. Thus, strictly speaking, a malum prohibitum offence, M, violates the wrongness constraint if there is even a single act token, *a*, falling within the definition of M such that *a* is not a moral wrong where *a* also admits of no relevant affirmative defence. In short, if the prohibited act type as defined is not *guaranteed* to amount to a wrong when unjustified, then the wrongness constraint strictly speaking is violated.

Very likely, many offence definitions carry some imprecision such that, despite the best efforts of drafters, there remains a small possibility of act tokens meeting the offence definition but that are not moral wrongs even when lacking an affirmative defence. This is due to natural human cognitive limitations and our inability to foresee every possible way the offence could be committed without falling within a defence. When such mistakes of overbreadth occur, as we suggested in Section 1, although the wrongness constraint strictly speaking is violated, this violation might very well be *excused* when the legislature used due care in how they drafted the relevant legal provisions. The greater the degree of conflict with the wrongness constraint (i.e. the more the offence sweeps in morally permissible act tokens), the greater the normative pressure on the legislature to amend the law to avoid the problem.

As a result, in real criminal law drafting, it is likely that some de minimis amount of conflict with the wrongness constraint might end up being tolerable – even if we insist on applying the constraint rigorously. Indeed, this might be reasonable particularly where other criminal law mechanisms can help avoid the injustice of such de minimis conflicts with the wrongness constraint. This might be through relying on either (1) prosecutorial discretion (e.g. finding that it is not in the public interest to prosecute particular act tokens[63]) or (2) sentencing discretion to impose minimal punishments that help minimise the residual unfairness of convicting someone who met the offence definition but did not act morally wrongly. Such safety valves might make drafters more comfortable tolerating small areas of conflict between a malum prohibitum offence and the wrongness constraint.

Practically, the normative pressure generated by the wrongness constraint against a malum prohibitum offence will be greater the *more pervasive* over-breadth it involves – that is, the more act tokens that meet the offence definition despite their being on balance morally permissible. The normative pressure against the offence will be further strengthened when prosecutorial discretion or similar safety valves are not sufficient to avoid any residual injustice from the over-broad offence. Thus, we will have the most worrisome conflicts with the wrongness constraint where the malum prohibitum offence both is *pervasively* over-broad in this way and fixes like prosecutorial discretion are not sufficient.[64]

Now note one additional wrinkle: if legislators face a particular malum prohibitum that seriously conflicts with the wrongness constraint in this way, this would not necessarily doom the offence and require striking it from the lawbooks. Instead, legislators could seek to *revise* the offence to remove the conflict. Such a revision could take one of two main forms. First, it could involve revising the offence elements to narrow its scope and thereby more tightly track the target set of act tokens that actually are moral wrongs when no defence applies. Second, it could involve expanding the scope of the applicable affirmative defences (e.g. expanding an existing justification or adding a new one – perhaps only for this offence) to better ensure that no act token is subject to conviction unless it is actually a moral wrong.

However, this latter move must be used with caution, as the presence of justificatory defences would still in principle allow one to be called into court and made to answer for the conduct one is accused of. Being called into court to answer is itself likely to be burdensome and anxiety-provoking even if one ultimately is exculpated through a defence – and so this posture should be used

---

[63] See e.g. *Code for Crown Prosecutors*, sections 4.9–4.10. Even when 'there is sufficient evidence to justify a prosecution ... prosecutors must go on to consider whether a prosecution is required in the public interest'.

[64] This is not to say it is of *no concern* if the over-breadth of the offence is not pervasive – only that it is a less pressing problem than widespread over-breadth.

sparingly. For conduct one is sure is not morally wrongful, the preferable solution is to avoid making it an offence in the first place.

When we are dealing with creating a *new* malum prohibitum offence that substantially conflicts with the wrongness constraint, then the remedial actions just described could easily be considered when shaping the offence and relevant statutory text. Thus, it may be easier to avoid substantial conflict with the wrongness constraint for newly proposed malum prohibitum offences than for existing ones. After all, when we are dealing with an *existing* malum prohibitum offence, it may be difficult to muster the political will to pass a new law amending an existing offence (which practitioners, courts, law enforcement and citizens may already be familiar with) so as to eliminate the conflict with the wrongness constraint.

Consequently, in assessing the extent to which insisting on a rigorous application of the wrongness constraint would require radical overhaul of the criminal law, we must focus not only on identifying the proportion of mala prohibita offences that *pervasively* or *substantially* conflict with the wrongness constraint, but also the extent to which *minimal revisions* to the law could remove this conflict. We take it that minimal revisions of this kind usually do not amount to a *radical* reform. This would help us reach an estimate of the extent to which a rigorous application of the wrongness constraint would necessitate widespread elimination of mala prohibita offences as opposed to just minor tweaks to offence definitions or defences.[65]

We speculate that when tweaks and fixes are accounted for, the degree of *radical* overhaul to the criminal law necessitated by rigorously applying the wrongness constraint would not in the end be massive. It may require widespread fixes via refined offence and defence definitions. But given the numerous legislative tools for resolving conflicts with the wrongness constraint, it is plausibly not an unmanageable degree of overhaul. If so, the current strategy of rigorously applying the wrongness constraint perhaps would not end up being unworkably radical after all.

What is more, even where a conflict with the wrongness constraint requires eliminating a given malum prohibitum (or several), the costs to the efficacy of a given regulatory scheme may not be so great when we recall the reasonable alternatives to mala prohibita crimes – such as civil liability or non-criminal fines. Accordingly, we wonder if it is not after all such a radical suggestion to

---

[65] One might wonder what the wrongness constraint would rule out given Youngjae Lee's suggestion, noted in Section 1, that offences have malum in se and mala prohibita components (Lee 2021). Would only 'pure' mala prohibita be excluded or also the 'mixed' malum in se/malum prohibitum offences? This is a good question, but general conclusions on this point are difficult to reach with confidence.

ask the legislature to rigorously apply the wrongness constraint. The degree of upheaval in both the criminal law and our ability to pursue worthwhile regulatory goals may not be so great as initially suspected.

The discussion thus far has assumed that mala prohibita offences likely involve substantial conflicts with the wrongness constraint. But it is time to revisit this assumption. The next section considers arguments for thinking that some mala prohibitum conduct is indeed morally wrongful for more subtle reasons than might have initially appeared. If these creative strategies succeed in establishing the moral wrongness of some malum prohibitum conduct, this would further lessen the conflict with the wrongness constraint – and thus the need for the reforms and alternatives considered in this section.

## 4 *Mala Prohibita* Really Are Wrongful

One way to reconcile mala prohibita with the wrongness constraint is to argue that it is indeed morally wrongful to commit the proscribed conduct. A leading way to do this is to argue for a moral obligation to obey the law. If there is a pro tanto moral obligation to obey the law, then there is a pro tanto duty to refrain from committing the mala prohibitum because the law has prohibited it.[66] This implies that it would be wrong to commit the mala prohibitum.

Whether there is a moral obligation to obey the law is among the oldest questions in philosophy, going as far back as the conversation between Socrates and Crito. One much-discussed issue is whether there is a *general* moral obligation of this sort, understood as a moral obligation to obey the law that is both *comprehensively applicable* and *universally borne* – that is, a moral obligation that everyone in the jurisdiction has to obey all the jurisdiction's norms (Kramer 2005: 180). Such a sweeping moral obligation to obey the law is seldom defended by contemporary theorists. This is because it seems implausible that there is a moral obligation to obey even patently unjust or immoral laws, and this seems to hold even if the obligation in question is only a pro tanto and defeasible one. Those who still defend a general moral obligation to obey the law nowadays do so only in narrower ways. Wellman (2013: 88), for example, contends that there is only a general moral obligation to obey the just laws of a legitimate state. Others, however, argue that there is no such general moral obligation to obey the law, not even when the law is (reasonably) just (e.g. Smith 1973; Raz 1979: 233–44). They doubt that any of the extant theories purporting to establish a moral obligation to obey successfully shows

---

[66] By 'obligation to *obey* the law', we simply refer to an obligation to do what the law requires that is (at least partly) grounded in the law saying so, and not the more demanding obligation to do what the law requires for the (motivating) reason that the law says so (see Hershovitz 2012: 65–75).

that the obligation to obey the law is a *general* one (see e.g. Simmons 1981). Rather, our obligations to obey the law vary from one person to the next and from one law to another depending on the circumstances (Raz 1979: 233–44, 1994: chapter 15).

Even if no extant theory establishes a general moral obligation to obey the law, this does not rule out establishing a moral obligation to obey *particular* mala prohibita or explaining why those particular actions are wrong. Rather than relying on a general moral obligation to obey to show that all mala prohibita (perhaps those of a just system) are wrongful, we can instead adopt a more piecemeal approach that seeks to show how there is a moral obligation to obey particular (or particular kinds of) mala prohibita rules. Indeed, most theorists who argue for the wrongfulness of mala prohibita adopt this more piecemeal approach in light of the difficulties for a general moral obligation to obey the law.

Given the voluminous literature on the subject, we will not provide a comprehensive survey of all possible accounts of the moral obligation to obey the law.[67] Rather, we focus only on those theories specifically advanced in relation to justifying mala prohibita crimes.[68] Traditionally, the most influential accounts that argue for the wrongfulness of mala prohibita in a piecemeal way include (explicit) consent, fair play and Rawls' natural duty to support just institutions (see e.g. Green 1997: 1577–89; Rawls 1971: 334). The latter also has contemporary defenders (Lee 2021: 431–2). We will consider these first before discussing some recent, more complex accounts.

## 4.1 Three Traditional Theories

### *4.1.1 Consent*

Examples of explicit consent include cases where people agree to obey certain legal rules or regulations in applying for a permit or licence to engage in certain activities (Green 1997: 1586). Thus, even if it is not inherently morally wrongful to violate those legal rules and regulations, it is now morally wrongful to do so because one agreed (understood as promising) to obey them.[69]

---

[67] For good critical surveys of the literature, see Horton 2010; Lefkowitz 2006; Edmundson 2004.

[68] Antje du Bois-Pedain (2014) advances an interesting view that we cannot explore due to limited space. On her view, the wrongfulness of some mala prohibita can perhaps be grounded in 'civility' (166–7).

[69] The terminology here can be confusing. Although typically referred to as 'consent' theories, these theories appeal to something more akin to promising than consent. The thought here is that one comes to have the obligation by promising or agreeing (in some sense) to being bounded by it. This contrasts with consent as when one consents to surgery, wherein one agrees to waive certain duties that others owe one.

One main difficulty with explicit consent is that while it shows how it is sometimes wrongful to violate certain mala prohibita, it fails to show that all instances of violating those mala prohibita are wrongful. Thus, for those who did not apply for a permit or licence to engage in the relevant activities, presumably we would want to say that it is still wrongful to violate the rules or regulations governing those activities. However, this cannot now be grounded in these actors' explicit consent since they never applied for the permit or licence and never agreed to obey the relevant rules in the process.

One way to avoid this problem is to appeal to 'tacit' consent. Tacit consent has historically been advanced to complement explicit consent to argue for a general obligation to obey the law. In its classical formulation, it holds that even if one has not made any explicit agreements to obey the law, one has nevertheless tacitly consented to do so by remaining in the country and using its services and infrastructures (Locke 1980: chapter 8, section 119). As the ground for a general obligation to obey the law, it suffers from at least two difficulties. First, it seems consent can be inferred from peoples' actions and behaviours only if they know they are tacitly consenting when they engage in those actions and behaviours. It seems unlikely that most people know that they are tacitly consenting to obeying the law simply by remaining in the country and using its services and infrastructures (Simmons 1976). This, of course, could be remedied (perhaps by setting up an institution that ensures everyone knows this by the time they are mature enough to give consent). However, second, even if people know they are tacitly consenting to obey by remaining in the country and using its services and infrastructure, we still cannot infer genuine consent from their actions since it is unreasonably costly for many to simply leave the country and/ or refrain from using its services and infrastructure.[70] The fact that they have remained and continued using the provided services and infrastructures therefore does not imply that they have freely consented to anything. Hume puts it best:

> Can we seriously say, that a poor peasant or artisan has a free choice to leave his country, when he knows no foreign language or manners, and lives, from day to day, by the small wages which he acquires? We may as well assert that a man, by remaining in a vessel, freely consents to the dominion of the master; though he was carried on board while asleep, and must leap into the ocean and perish, the moment he leaves her. (1752)

While this might be fatal for establishing a general obligation to obey the law, it is less problematic for a piecemeal approach that only seeks to establish an

---

[70] What is more, someone who leaves one jurisdiction will just find herself in another, and so very likely will be unable to escape legal control altogether (Dworkin 1998: 193).

obligation to obey particular mala prohibita. This is especially the case for the kinds of mala prohibita governing specific activities. This can range from specialised activities like waste disposal, to fishing in a certain rivers, to everyday activities like driving. It seems plausible to think that it is not unreasonably costly for one to avoid engaging in at least some of these activities, either because it is highly specialised and not essential to one's life (e.g. waste disposal or leisure fishing – the same cannot be said for fishing if one's livelihood depends on it), or is essential to one's life but reasonable alternatives exist (e.g. affordable and effective public transport as an alternative to driving). If so, and if adequate notice can be given that one tacitly consents to obeying the relevant regulations when one engages in the activities in question (which arguably is easier if the activity is geographically bounded, like fishing in a certain stretch of the river), then it seems tacit consent can be a plausible basis for the obligation to obey these particular mala prohibita regulations, even for those who have never explicitly agreed to do so.

Nevertheless, even if tacit consent helps to complement explicit consent, it is still doubtful whether those who have consented explicitly or tacitly do indeed have an obligation to obey all the relevant regulations. Normally for an agreement to be binding, one needs to know what exactly one is agreeing to. This implies that one must have sufficient knowledge of the relevant regulations that govern the activity in question before one can have an obligation to obey all of them based on consent. This does not seem practically feasible if the activity is governed by many persnickety rules and regulations. It also seems to imply that new agreements need to be sought whenever there are changes to the rules and regulations. One way to avoid such practical problems is to resort to more generic agreements like 'I hereby agree to conform to all the provisions within XXX Act and any future amendments to it'; but again it is questionable whether such generic agreements do bind one to obey all the rules and regulations within the Act and all subsequent amendments to it when one does not know all of them in detail when one made the agreement.

There are further difficulties with grounding the wrongfulness of mala prohibita on explicit and tacit consent. As Husak explains, many of these agreements to abide by the relevant laws can be described as like 'boilerplate' contracts or 'contracts of adhesion' that are offered on a 'take-it-or-leave-it' basis where those who are asked to consent have less bargaining power over the terms of the agreement than those who set out the agreement. This, one might argue, undermines the bindingness of the agreement. Finally, even if the wrongfulness of certain mala prohibita can be adequately accounted for by explicit and/or tacit consent, one might still wonder how promising this strategy would be for the purpose of justifying criminalisation since contract and promise breaking are normally not criminalised (Husak 2005: 83–4). Why would this kind of promise to obey certain rules plausibly merit punishment when this is not done for other kinds of promise breaking?

### 4.1.2 Fair Play

According to the principle of fair play (at least the version in Hart (1955: 185–6); we explore other versions later), insofar as one has benefitted from others' submission to a set of rules or regulations, then one owes it to others to similarly submit to those rules or regulations. Refusing to do so would be to free ride on the efforts and sacrifices of others. Accordingly, assuming that one has benefitted from, for example, the safety provided by others' obedience to the regulations concerning annual car inspections, then one owes it to others to obey those regulations as well.[71] It would therefore be morally wrongful for one to violate those regulations, even if one does not in fact endanger anyone in doing so and somehow knows this to be the case.

It is important to distinguish fair play from a closely related notion: cheating. Cheating, according to Green, consists in 'rule-breaking intended to obtain an unfair advantage over another with whom one is in a cooperative, rule-bound relationship'; and this, Green (2006: 250–1) argues, is precisely what is morally wrongful with some mala prohibita violations. We have no doubt that some violations of mala prohibita involve cheating in this sense and are therefore morally wrongful. However, much mala prohibitum conduct can also be committed without the requisite intention. After all, the intention to obtain an unfair advantage is not typically an element in mala prohibita offences nor is proof thereof required for conviction. Cheating (as understood by Green) therefore can only offer a rather limited account of the wrongfulness of mala prohibita – it is morally wrongful for someone to commit them only if they do so with the requisite intention. Fair play, by contrast, does not hold that it is morally wrongful to commit a malum prohibitum in virtue of one's intention to take unfair advantage, but in virtue of how the rule-breaking actually involves taking unfair advantage of others, regardless of one's intention to take advantage or not. Fair play therefore is not limited in the same way as cheating.

However, like explicit consent, fair play also suffers from the problem that not all instances of violating the same malum prohibitum are wrongful on fair-play grounds. One classic criticism of the version of the principle of fair play we

---

[71] This example was drawn from Lee (2022a: 385). Another example he offers is paying taxes. For another, see Green 1997: 1589–90. For criticisms of Green's example, see Husak 2005: 88–9. Other helpful examples include storing or disposing of hazardous waste without a permit and selling unregistered securities.

have been looking at is that *merely receiving a benefit* is insufficient to generate a fair play duty to do one's fair share (which in our case is to obey the malum prohibitum like everyone else).[72] Rather, as Simmons (1979) argues, one must have also *accepted the benefit* in question before one can have that duty of fair play. Accordingly, at least for those who have not accepted the benefits of the malum prohibitum in question, it cannot be morally wrongful for them to violate that malum prohibitum for reasons of fair play.

Still, as with explicit consent, we must be careful not to overstate the problem this poses for a piecemeal approach that only seeks to establish a fair-play-based obligation to obey particular mala prohibita. To have accepted a benefit, according to Simmons, is to have either (1) tried to get the benefit in question (and succeeded) or (2) taken the benefit willingly while knowing its nature as a product of a cooperative enterprise with associated burdens (Simmons 1979: 327–30).[73] It seems plausible that at least some mala prohibita (e.g. regulations for ensuring sustainable fishing) are such that simply by engaging in the relevant activity (e.g. fishing in the designated areas) one has thereby accepted, in the sense of (1), the benefit provided by such mala prohibita. However, for other mala prohibita (e.g. regulations governing waste disposal or annual car inspections) one need not (so to speak) 'go out of one's way' to obtain the benefit of such regulations, but these benefits are instead 'open' to all and cannot be easily avoided. In such cases, a lot then depends on whether those who violate those mala prohibita have really *accepted* the benefits of them in the sense described in (2).[74] To the extent they have not, such offenders still have not acted wrongfully on fair play grounds.

Note that while Simmons' characterisation of this 'acceptance condition' is widely accepted, it is not ecumenical. Dagger (1997) argues that Simmons' view of 'acceptance' is too narrow. He contends that by requiring individuals to have at least taken the benefit willingly and knowingly in the sense of (2) before they incur an obligation based on fair play, this 'rule[s] out many cases in which we attribute obligations to individuals who have not deliberately – that is, *with actual deliberation* – incurred those obligations' (75). Dagger argues we should see individuals as 'growing into' the political community in which they are born, rather than being 'dropped into' it (a view he attributes to Simmons). It is through such 'growing into' that they come to accept the benefits provided and therefore incur an obligation based on fair play even when they have not

---

[72] For a classic argument for this, see Nozick 1974: 93.

[73] Note that 'acceptance' in this sense is different from consent. Simmons' (1979: 325–6) fair play principle therefore does not simply collapse into the consent theory.

[74] For what it means to accept in the sense of (2) benefits that are 'open' in this way, see Simmons 1979: 329–30.

undertaken them 'with full awareness and conscious intent' (75). Dagger puts it thus:

> [T]he political order qua cooperative enterprise is indeed something that most of us do not choose to join, but it is not something foreign to us. . . . Perhaps we merely receive these benefits when we are infants and youngsters, but as we grow older and gradually learn something about how our political community operates, most of us begin to take advantage of the opportunities the community offers to pursue our interests. We use public transportation; we begin to drive a car; we apply for admission to a public university or seek a state funded scholarship; we vote in an election; we enter into a contract; [etc]. In doing these things—in *growing into* membership in the polity—we accept the benefits of the political order *qua* cooperative enterprise and undertake an obligation to obey its laws. (76–7)

Broadening the acceptance condition in this way makes it easier for fair play to capture the wrongfulness of mala prohibita. Whether that is a plausible account, however, will depend on whether one accepts Dagger's argument about how we can come to undertake a fair play obligation even when we do not do so 'with full awareness and conscious intent'. It also depends on whether one accepts as plausible his view about individuals 'growing into' the political community: whether that view, for example, squares well with mass migration and the cosmopolitan features of many modern societies. Still, one distinctive aspect of Dagger's view is his appeal to political theory in his fair play argument for an obligation to obey the law. A political theory that at least sketches the kind of relationship that individuals have with each other, their political communities and their laws (i.e. that according to Dagger they 'grow into' their political communities rather than being 'dropped into' them). Whether one accepts the particular picture Dagger sketches, as we will see in discussing Duff's civic responsibility view in Section 4.2.3, there is a growing recognition of the importance and indispensability of political theory when thinking about the wrongfulness of mala prohibita.[75] We will draw out some of the implications of this in discussing Duff.

Another response to Simmons' acceptance condition for fair play is to deny it in certain kinds of cases.[76] Klosko (2005: 6) argues that at least when it comes to benefits that are 'open' (which Klosko calls 'nonexcludable goods'), the mere receipt of those benefits can give rise to obligations based on fair play if (1) it is worth the recipient's effort in providing them, (2) those benefits are indispensable for satisfactory lives, and (3) the benefits and burdens of the cooperative scheme are fairly distributed.

---

[75] And about criminalisation and the criminal law more generally (see e.g. Ristroph 2011a).

[76] For a critical discussion of other responses that fall within this camp, see Simmons 2001: chapter 2.

One question is whether an acceptance condition for fair play is indeed irrelevant when Klosko's three conditions are met (see e.g. Simmons 1987: 270–5). But even so, Klosko's version of fair play still suffers from a limitation in accounting for the wrongfulness of mala prohibita. The difficulty is mainly with condition (2) (though it can also be extended to (1)). While many of our mala prohibita are aimed at protecting people from harm and in that sense provide a benefit that is 'indispensable for satisfactory lives', not all of them can plausibly be understood in this way. Take the offence of money laundering discussed by Husak (2005: 67). It does not seem plausible to think that somehow people would be unable to lead satisfactory lives simply because we do not forbid people from engaging in monetary transactions involving what they know or suspect are ill-gotten gains. Instead, it is more plausible that such an offence makes it easier and more effective to detect and prosecute people for committing more serious offences that do indeed undermine people's ability to lead satisfactory lives (e.g. human trafficking and other violent crimes). Thus, as long as these more serious offences are still adequately enforced without the money-laundering offence, then Klosko's condition (2) is not met as the latter offence is not strictly speaking providing a benefit that is '*indispensable* for a satisfactory life'.

In other words, as long as a malum prohibitum is not itself necessary for people to lead satisfactory lives, but merely makes it more efficient to ensure that people are able to do so, either by reducing its costs and burdens or serving as a 'proxy crime' to make it easier to detect and prosecute more serious and harmful crimes (see Lee 2022b), then not all of Klosko's three conditions are met. This implies that there is no fair-play-based obligation to obey the malum prohibitum unless one has accepted the benefits that it provides. This then takes us back to the original problem with using fair play to account for the wrongfulness of mala prohibita: not all instances of violating a particular malum probihitum rule are wrongful, as the wrongness of some such violations will depend on whether one has accepted the associated benefits. That said, Klosko's version of fair play is a slight improvement than before as under his view, at least some mala prohibita (i.e. those that do satisfy all three of his conditions) would not suffer from this problem, when before they did.

Klosko (2005: 102–5) wants to establish a general obligation to obey the law and is aware of this limitation to his fair play argument. Thus, Klosko supplements his version of fair play with a 'Natural Duty Principle' and a 'Common Good Principle'. Klosko thinks all these notions, when taken together, establish a general obligation to obey the law (105–20). However, Klosko's arguments notwithstanding, the general obligation to obey the law remains highly controversial, and our focus in any case is the piecemeal approach to accounting for the wrongfulness of mala prohibita. That said, the other attempts that we examine in the rest of this section, namely Rawls' natural duty to support just institutions and Duff's civic responsibility approach, have close affinities with Klosko's 'Natural Duty Principle' and 'Common Good Principle'. So the concerns faced by those attempts also apply to these additional elements of Klosko's view.

### 4.1.3 Rawls' Natural Duty to Support Just Institutions

Rawls (1971: 334) contends that within 'the theory of justice, the most important natural duty is that to support and to further just institutions'. The most important component of this duty for our purposes is the requirement 'to comply with and to do our share in just institutions when they exist and apply to us'. If Rawls is right, then we have a moral obligation to obey mala prohibita at least if they are part of a just institution.

There is, of course, the question of when a set of legal regulations is just.[77] But even setting this aside, there is still a whiff of circularity if one simply appeals to this Rawlsian natural duty to argue for the wrongfulness of mala prohibita: why is it morally wrong to engage in the prohibited conduct? Because we simply have a natural duty to abide by those rules when they are just seems hardly a satisfying answer.

To be clear, we *do not deny* that there is a general duty to support just institutions. What we think is missing here, however, is an argument showing how this general duty to support just institutions implies that there is a moral obligation to abide by just mala prohibita and thus it is morally wrongful to perform the prohibited conduct.[78] Consider, therefore, the following argument: plausibly, this general duty includes or implies at least a negative duty not to *undermine* just institutions and their attempts to pursue just causes (unless, that is, there are overriding reasons to the contrary). On this basis, one might argue that it is wrong to commit a malum prohibitum (that is itself just or a part of a just set of legal regulations) because in doing so one undermines the regulations in question and the just causes that they seek to promote.

---

[77] For Rawls' own famous answer to this, see Rawls 1971: part 1.

[78] By 'just mala prohibita', we mean mala prohibita that are justifiably enacted (e.g. that they serve important enough ends in a proportionate and fair way) and not simply laws issued by a just institution. The question is how to get an argument from the more general duty to support just institutions to the more granular claim that it is wrongful to violate any justifiably enacted malum prohibitum offence. Note also that although they are closely related, the duty to support just institutions is subtly different from a general obligation to obey the law. For example, it is at least conceptually possible one can satisfy one's duty of support even without full-on obedience to the law's requirements in all cases.

The problem with this argument is similar to the difficulty discussed before: it does not show all instances of violating the mala prohibita in question are wrongful. This is because not all instances of law breaking would undermine the legal institution in question and the goods it aims to promote. Thus, not all violations of mala prohibita that are part of just institutions are wrongful in virtue of violating the duty to support just institutions if we are to simply understand this duty as a negative one. One reason for this is the familiar fact that any given legal institution can tolerate a certain level of non-compliance as long as the majority complies most of the time (Wellman 2001: 748–9; Wellman and Simmons 2005: 168–70). But we can also see this in less morally suspect cases involving hybrid mala prohibita that are intentionally over-inclusive. Think, for example, of the expert pharmacist who uses ingredients from a list of legally banned dangerous substances but in doing so did not put anyone at risk because of her superior expert knowledge. Given that this pharmacist did not commit the wrong that is targeted by such a malum prohibitum, and has not caused the harms it seeks to prevent, it is unclear in what way she has, in failing to comply with the regulations against using these legally banned substances, undermined the just cause that such regulations aim to achieve. Therefore, it is unclear why it would violate her negative duty to support such institutions by not undermining them.

Of course, the pharmacist would arguably be violating her negative duty to not undermine such institutions if she goes around encouraging others (especially those with less expertise) not to comply with those regulations. But then in that case it is her encouragement of others to not comply with the regulations, not her non-compliance therewith, that violates her negative duty to not undermine just institutions and is accordingly morally wrongful.

One possibility is that even if the pharmacist does not go around encouraging others, her non-compliance (if known to others) would set an example of non-compliance for others to follow, and in this way indirectly undermine the just cause that the regulations aim to achieve. The problem with this pro-Rawlsian response is that non-compliance would only be wrongful if it is publicly known and is taken by others as an example to follow.[79] Thus, again, not all instances of non-compliance would be morally wrongful because it involves violating one's duty to not undermine just institutions. More importantly, however, even if one's non-compliance does have such an effect, it is unclear that one should be blameworthy and be held responsible for the wrongful choices that others make, especially when one did not set oneself up as an example for others to follow in

---

[79] Indeed, in some cases, it is precisely because we hold the law breaker to public account that her non-compliance becomes public knowledge.

the first place. The fact that it was the result of others' choices seems to constitute a novus actus interveniens here.

In fairness, what is causing the difficulty here is understanding the duty to support just institutions simply as a negative duty to not undermine them. One might therefore argue that such difficulties can be avoided if this duty is understood not simply as a negative one, but also a positive one that requires abiding by the just rules and regulations set out by the just institution. The trick then is to argue for this in a way that does not beg the question in relation to the wrongfulness of mala prohibita. We will consider one such attempt at doing this in the next section. But before that, and by way of laying the groundwork for it, we will first consider one recent more sophisticated attempt to account for the wrongfulness of mala prohibita by combining fair play with the natural duty idea.

## 4.2 Moving beyond the Traditional Theories

### 4.2.1 Samaritanism: Combining Fair Play and Natural Duty

The main problem for the three traditional theories discussed is that while each of them can show why some instances of committing a certain malum prohibitum are morally wrongful, they fail to show that *all* instances of doing so are morally wrongful. This is because, for explicit consent, it is wrongful only for those who have consented to obeying the malum prohibitum; for those who accept an acceptance condition for fair play, it is wrongful only for those who have accepted the associated benefits; and for the natural duty to support just institutions understood in a purely negative way, not all instances of non-compliance undermine the just cause promoted by the institution into which the malum prohibitum figures.

Accordingly, one promising strategy is to combine the traditional accounts to 'plug the gaps' described. One view pursuing this strategy is Wellman's Samaritanism, which combines elements from fair play and the natural duty tradition (Wellman 2001, 2013: 77–96). Rather than a Rawlsian natural duty to support just institutions, Wellman relies on the natural duty to help others in peril (hence the name 'Samaritanism'). The idea is this: we all have a natural duty to help others in peril when it is not unreasonably costly to do so. Accordingly, if obeying a set of laws is not unreasonably costly and helps alleviate others from peril (e.g. the perils of the state of nature), then it would be morally wrongful for us to not do so on account of our Samaritan duty, even when it is not independently morally wrongful to perform the prohibited conduct in itself. However, since we all have this Samaritan duty, it is therefore unfair for one to refuse to bear this burden to obey that others have borne in fulfilling it. One would be free riding on the efforts of others. It is therefore morally wrongful for one to disobey the laws in question, even if one's disobedience does not have any discernible effect of undermining the institution in question. As Wellman (2013) argues,

> [E]ach citizen has a duty to obey the law as his or her fair share of the collective political task. Thus, if states are justified because they perform the incredibly important task of rescuing all of us from the perils of the state of nature, then each of us has a duty to obey the law as his or her fair share of this larger communal project ... [E]ven if there were no discrete harms that followed from [one's] legal disobedience, he or she would be taking unfair advantage of his or her fellow citizens. (85)

In this way, fair play helps to 'plug the gaps' left by the appeal to natural duty here. As Wellman (2001: 749) admits, '[A]ny given citizen's behavior typically has no discernible effect on her state's capacity to perform its functions, and thus it is descriptively inaccurate to suggest that one's obedience to the law is necessary to secure important benefits ... (even Samaritan benefits).' However, appealing to a natural duty (more specifically, the Samaritan duty to help others in peril) as the fundamental ground helps to show why at least this particular fair play moral obligation to obey is not plausibly subjected to an acceptance condition. This is because as a natural duty, 'samaritan responsibilities bind all, not just those who consent to or accept them' (Wellman 2001: 750). Putting all this together, according to Samaritanism, insofar as obeying a certain malum prohibitum helps to alleviate others from peril and is not unreasonably costly, then it is morally wrongful to disobey it because in doing so one fails to undertake a fair share of one's Samaritan duty to help others in peril.

Many questions can be raised about Samaritanism and whether it offers a plausible argument for an obligation to obey the law (see e.g. Wellman and Simmons 2005: 179–88). Even if it does, it is clear that there is a limit to how far Samaritanism can show it is morally wrongful to violate mala prohibita. The issue here is similar to the limitation that Klosko's view of fair play suffers from and arises because of the particular natural duty that Wellman's view relies on. The Samaritan duty is only triggered in cases where others are in *peril* or would be in *peril* had one not intervened. Thus, similar to what we discussed in relation to Klosko's 'indispensable benefits', we can imagine a malum prohibitum (e.g. the anti-money-laundering offence discussed before) that is not itself necessary to protect people from serious harm or from falling into some kind of peril, but merely makes it more efficient or effective to do so. This could be, for example, by serving as a 'proxy crime' that makes it easier to detect and prosecute more serious crimes that do imperil others. Accordingly, it seems there cannot be an obligation to obey the malum prohibitum in question according to Samaritanism. This is because such as it is, the malum prohibitum is not consequential enough to trigger the Samaritan duty. Thus, just like Klosko's argument for a fair-play-based but acceptance-independent moral obligation to obey the law, the Samaritan argument for the wrongfulness of mala prohibita may not extend very far.

How problematic this is will depend on how many mala prohibita are actually not necessary to protect people from serious harm or other perils, and therefore are not consequential enough to trigger the Samaritan duty. Generally speaking, if it turns out that vast numbers of mala prohibita are not consequential enough to trigger the Samaritan duty, then so much the worse for Samaritanism as a way to reconcile mala prohibita with the wrongness constraint (assuming such offences are a defensible part of the criminal law).

Like Klosko, Wellman is acutely aware of this limitation to Samaritanism.[80] In response to the objection that Samaritanism can only justify a 'minimal, "night-watcher" state' and not a 'full-blown, liberal welfare state', the latter of which includes the state performing 'various administrative functions (such as regulating the commodities markets ...), which clearly do not rescue people from perilous circumstances', Wellman argues that other grounds can be combined with Samaritanism to justify these 'more extensive political functions' (Wellman 2001: 7578). One such ground, Wellman argues, is democracy. This is because 'while samaritanism justifies the existence of a political state, citizens could rightfully object to being subjected to the laws of an undemocratic state. If so, then the moral demands of democracy might justify many political functions which samaritanism alone would not' (758).

Wellman's remarks on democracy are not directed at mala prohibita specifically. They are also rather brief and speculative. Nevertheless, we find it plausible that democracy, even when not combined with Samaritanism, can be a possible ground for the wrongfulness of certain mala prohibita. After all, many examples of mala prohibita that we have looked at are democratically enacted and it would be surprising if the democratic process has no role to play in why it is wrong to violate the resulting laws. Nevertheless, the issue of why (and when) it is wrong to break democratically created laws, has received comparatively less attention, especially by mainstream legal theorists working on issues of criminalisation. Even where democracy is acknowledged (e.g. in Wellman's account and, as seen in Section 4.2.3, in Duff's), it is still not

---

[80] At least in 2001 where he used Samaritanism to argue for a general obligation to obey the law. Interestingly, in 2013, he does not mention this limitation when he specifically discussed Samaritanism in relation to mala prohibita.

something that is given a detailed treatment.[81] There seems to be something of a lacuna in the literature here, on the role of democracy and the wrongfulness of conduct proscribed through democratic processes.

### 4.2.2 A Revised Hybrid View: Combining Fair Play with Rawlsian Natural Duty

Given the limitations of Samaritanism, some might opt not to rely on Wellman's limited Samaritan duty, but rather on a broader Rawlsian duty to support just institutions. Combining this with fair play, the revised view then is that insofar as the malum prohibitum in question is (or is a part of) a just institution serving a just cause, then it is morally wrongful to disobey and violate the malum prohibitum because in doing so one fails to undertake a fair share of one's duty to support just institutions. Call this the 'Rawlsian Hybrid View'.

The Rawlsian Hybrid View does not suffer from the limitation of Samaritanism because the natural duty it employs is not limited to cases of peril. Combining fair play with Rawls' natural duty to support just institutions can also explain why it is not simply a negative duty to not undermine just institutions and the just causes they pursue, but also a positive duty to do one's part in supporting those institutions and causes. Obeying the rules and regulations that are needed for these just causes is not a burden that should only be borne by some, but a fair burden that we should all undertake as part of doing our part in supporting just institutions and their just causes. Failing to abide by them, even when it does not undermine the just institution and their just causes, is morally wrongful because one fails to do one's part in this collective endeavour.

Despite these advantages, we still worry that this Rawlsian duty to support just institutions, even when combined with fair play, is simply too broad and abstract a duty to provide a persuasive argument for the moral wrongfulness of specific mala prohibita. As we discussed before, we do think there is a general duty to support just institutions, and this includes at least a defeasible negative duty to not undermine just institutions and their attempts to pursue just causes. However, the Rawlsian Hybrid View does not simply ask for our forbearance and non-interference. It asks us to do our part to positively support just institutions, more specifically by obeying the malum prohibitum in question. But it is a legitimate question why we owe just institutions positive support and not just non-interference and forbearance, and why this positive support needs to take the form of obeying their rules (rather than other kinds of support). It seems

---

[81] For a recent critical discussion of the main positions in the literature on this issue, see Viehoff 2014.

implausible to think that this is simply because it is a just institution pursuing a just cause. Just because someone or some group of people take up a just cause does not mean that we now have a duty to support them and their cause by obeying the rules that they set down. At a minimum, we are owed an explanation of why we all have a proper role to play in pursuing this just cause, why it is fair to expect and demand that we fulfil this role, and why that role involves obeying the rules that have been set down.

Consider the expert pharmacist whose superior knowledge enables her to use legally banned dangerous substances safely, or the mechanic who does not do MOT tests for her car because she services her car regularly. The just cause that the regulations in these cases serve is obvious: their purpose is to protect the public from the serious harms caused by unsafe uses of dangerous substances and unsafe cars on the road. It is also clear why this should involve obeying those particular rules, at least for those who are unable to use those substances safely or regularly service their cars properly. However, for the expert pharmacist and mechanic, who *ex hypothesi* know what they are doing and are not putting anyone at risk, why is it also their part to obey those same rules and regulations? Why is it fair to expect and demand that they do the same as those lacking special knowledge who would be putting others at risk?

The point is not that there can never be adequate answers to these questions. Rather, the point is simply that the Rawlsian Hybrid View is incomplete, since it only speaks in abstract terms of our general duty to support just institutions and doing our fair share of it. What is needed is a further story about why we *all* have a fair and proper role to play, which involves obeying the mala prohibita in question, even when our disobedience would not undermine the just cause.

### 4.2.3 Duff and Civic Responsibilities

One such further story is offered by Duff. He thinks we must look at the civic responsibilities that we, as citizens, have in relation to each other and the common good of the polity. Insofar as the malum prohibitum under consideration is ultimately grounded in the civic responsibilities that citizens have to each other, then it would be wrong not to abide by it, even when this does not undermine the common good in question (or the 'just cause', as we put it). This is because in doing so, we fail to fulfil our civic responsibilities and thus fail to do our part as fellow members of the polity.

For example, Duff asks us to consider a driver who knows she can safely drive above the speed limit or knows she can safely drive when she is above the drink drive limit. Assume that the burden for obeying these legal limits is relatively light; that such blanket rules are significantly more effective in reducing harmful behaviour than ones that allow for exemptions; and that there are considerable costs to allowing a formal defence for drivers who know what they are doing will not endanger others. In such cases, Duff argues that drivers who do know they can drive safely above the legal limits nevertheless ought to obey those limits and not seek an exception for themselves out of solidarity with their fellow citizens (Duff 2018: 319–20). Duff goes on to apply this 'civic responsibility' approach to 'preemptive offences', some of which are arguably mala prohibita (324–32).[82] These include offences of possessing information that is likely to be useful for others to commit serious crimes, offences of failure to report actual or suspected criminal activity and criminal regulations against gun possession. Duff argues that it can be wrong to commit these offences due to a range of civic responsibilities, including to make sure we do not assist others in their criminal enterprises (not simply to refrain from purposely aiding them), to pay attention to the actions of our fellow citizens (not only to the effects of our own actions), and to 'provide assurance of trustworthiness' that our fellow citizens are entitled to (331).[83]

It is important to note that Duff does not conclusively assert that we actually *have* these civic responsibilities. Rather, his point is that the wrongfulness of various mala prohibita can be accounted for by our civic responsibilities, and that we can establish their wrongfulness by figuring out what civic responsibilities we owe each other as fellow citizens. Duff puts it this way regarding offences of failures to report:

> [M]y aim is not to answer such questions as these [whether we have the civic responsibility in question and whether it should be turned into a legal duty]. It is ... that to answer such questions we must ... work out an important dimension of our civil order, concerning the kinds of civic responsibility we should have, as citizens, to pay practical attention not just to the effects of our actions ..., but also to the actions of our fellow citizens – and the ways in which such responsibilities should be qualified or limited by the regard that we should also have for the privacy and the freedom of those fellow citizens. (327)

According to Duff then, what is needed to properly account for the wrongfulness of mala prohibita is nothing short of a political theory that describes the kind of relationship that we ought to have with each other as fellow citizens, and the responsibilities we owe one another and their limits. For Duff, this is

---

[82] Duff also applies this approach to preparatory offences, but those are not mala prohibita. If it is wrong to commit a crime, then it is also wrong to prepare to commit it. The issue with preparatory offences is instead when preparing to commit an offence becomes sufficiently wrong to merit legal intervention.

[83] The latter can include not just that we act in trustworthy ways, but that we provide formal and public assurances thereof. More on this later.

a matter of 'political morality', 'in the sense that it is a morality that is developed and articulated as a collective enterprise by the polity and its members (in a well functioning democratic polity): it is the morality under which they are to live together as citizens' (311). Accordingly, it is not something 'that can be answered through individual reflection on morality', but 'can be adequately tackled only through public deliberation about the kind of polity that we are to construct for ourselves' (324).

Although it is ultimately a matter of public deliberation, it is still possible to discern in general terms some of the civic responsibilities we might have in virtue of being members of a liberal democratic society. In relation to gun possession offences, Duff thinks it is a proper aim of a 'democratic republic to find ways in which its citizens can be assured, and can reassure each other', which can include regulations that 'specify the formal procedures through which the necessary assurances can be provided' (331). The thought here is that we have a general civic responsibility to provide (re-)assurance of trustworthiness to one another as fellow citizens, but what exactly this requires of us is a matter of public deliberation – a deliberation that takes into account how our need for shared civic understandings require formal procedures for providing such assurances, as well as how much (perceived) security we can demand from the polity and each other, and how much (perceived) insecurity we are willing to accept. Other civic responsibilities, however, will depend on the specific kind of liberal democratic society that we see ourselves as members of. Thus, the idea that we ought to obey certain mala prohibita out of solidarity with our fellow citizens is, Duff admits, more plausible for those who (like him) hold a 'communitarian conception of citizenship' than for those with more 'individualist leanings' (320).

Limited space prevents a more detailed examination of Duff's sophisticated view. Instead, two points in conclusion. On Duff's 'civic responsibility' approach, accounting for the wrongfulness of mala prohibita involves articulating and defending an underlying political theory that outlines (1) the general kinds of civic responsibilities to each other, and (2) how these are given concrete content through public deliberation. This implies, unlike the approaches considered earlier, that we should not expect to find one master principle or principles (e.g. fair play, consent and/or some natural duty) that we can apply straightforwardly to determine the wrongfulness of various mala prohibita. Rather, it will inevitably be a more piecemeal process. The second implication is the indispensability of political theory when thinking about the wrongfulness of mala prohibita. It is, so to speak, a matter of 'political morality' and not simply a matter of morality between private individuals considered in isolation from their membership in a political community. Duff's view belongs to a growing number of views that see political theory as key to understanding the wrongfulness of mala prohibita (and criminalisation generally). The underlying political theory that Duff relies on is a kind of communitarian liberal republicanism (Duff 2018: chapter 5), but one can conceivably endorse a different political theory instead (see e.g. Dagger 2016; Dimock 2014).

Let us quickly take stock. This section seeks to reconcile mala prohibita with the wrongness constraint by arguing that it is indeed morally wrongful to commit the proscribed conduct. We began by looking at the obligation to obey the law and some traditional accounts of it, but they were found wanting. Critically engaging with Wellman's Samaritanism, which combines certain traditional accounts in order to avoid their respective inadequacies, led us to Duff's 'civic responsibility' approach. While promising, this approach is also demanding to apply in order to generate verdicts about specific mala prohibita: according to this approach, properly accounting for the wrongfulness of mala prohibita requires us to argue for nothing short of a political theory that outlines the civic responsibilities we have towards our fellow citizens and the role of public deliberation in determining them.

## 4.3 Public Justifiability and the Wrongfulness of *Mala Prohibita*

We end this section by considering a recent argument for the wrongfulness of mala prohibita that is less demanding in many ways. It builds on a recent contribution from Simester. The idea is that the reasons supporting a justified regulatory scheme, of which a given malum prohibitum offence is part, can *indirectly* count against the malum prohibitum conduct itself, thus rendering it morally wrong (Simester 2021: 240–2).[84] Note that in pursuing this argument, we are not rejecting Duff's civic responsibility approach. Rather, our development of Simester's view can complement and work alongside Duff's view in accounting for the wrongfulness of mala prohibita.

Let us sketch Simester's argument before we expand it. He focuses on a core kind of case of mala prohibita that we have looked at earlier: those that are part of a regulatory regime that is assumed to be justified, but where an actor has special knowledge or expertise that enables them to be highly confident (and justifiably so) that they will not bring about the harms or dangers that the regulatory scheme aims to prevent. In such cases, there is a worry that because

---

[84] This builds on his earlier work (Simester and von Hirsch 2011). Simester's earlier argument was somewhat different in contending that if the state justifiably exercises its authority to prohibit φ, then it is morally wrong for one to φ (Simester 2011: 24–9). However, for present purposes this is not entirely satisfying, as some explanation is needed of what grounds the state's authority to make it morally wrong to φ when it justifiably prohibits φ. In fact, the theories this section considered are attempts to provide just such an explanation.

the underpinning regulatory goals are not threatened, it may seem not to be morally wrong for the expert to violate the relevant malum prohibitum rule. To anchor the discussion, let us return to the case of Rhea from Section 1. Recall that she was the expert chemist who knew how to safely dispose of hazardous waste for mining companies and commenced a perfectly safe disposal process without first obtaining the required licence. Rhea has committed a crime. While she likely behaved imprudently, let us set aside self-interest for now (perhaps Rhea's offence will not be detected). But why has she done something that is morally wrong? That is the puzzle we want answered. Simester (2021) explains his solution as follows:

> The constraints imposed by limited state resources and practicalities of enforcement may ... entail that individual nuances cannot be evaluated, legally, on an ad hoc basis. Implementing a practicable system for [pursuing worthy regulatory goals] may depend on upon the state's not having to set aside the resources to make personalized claims of difference justiciable. In turn, provided the burden imposed by the regime is not unduly onerous, and the benefits it secures are sufficiently valuable, we may conclude that D ought to conform to its requirements; that there is no sufficient reason why D is entitled to special consideration. (241)

Simester is alive to the worry that even if the regulatory scheme is in general justified, one might still wonder why this should constrain an expert like Rhea who is certain not to cause the dangers the scheme aims to prevent. Simester replies:

> There is ... a public interest in enforcing and protecting [the regulatory] regime, derived [from the] harm involved in unsafe mixing of the chemicals. Admittedly, D [herself] poses no risk of such harm. But ... to allow D exceptional treatment *modifies the regime itself*. D can either (a) get a licence or (b) claim to be different. But the latter claim will need to be tested too, via some form of trial or administrative inquiry ... Moreover, option (b) must then be available in principle to everyone else, since we don't know in advance whether any particular person is such an expert. The result is significantly increased expense, which comes out of the public purse: accommodating D's claim thus deprives others of the resources that are needlessly used up by D. **If that's right, it follows that D has moral reasons to pursue option (a) and get the licence.** (242)

The last sentence (in bold) is the key move. From the observation that an expert's claim to be exempted from the licensing requirement would have to be tested through a system that is open to anyone else (making it more costly to the public purse), Simester concludes that the expert *herself* has moral reasons to give up her desired exemption and instead get the licence like anyone else.

Still questions remain. Just because there are good reasons *for the state* not to create a system for evaluating requests for exemptions to its regulatory requirements – including both the cost and the need to ensure equal access for all to the system – why would it follow that an *individual* actor's reasons get affected, such that she herself has moral reason to actually comply with the regulatory requirement? How is it that the *state's reasons*, pertaining to institutional design and resource allocation, affect the individual actor's reasons for how to act in this context? We want a fuller story about *how*, exactly, the individual's reasons get affected by the state's reasons (including reasons of affordability and budgeting).

Thus, for all that has been said so far, it's unclear why the following two claims cannot both be true:

(1) the state may legitimately decide not to incur the costs of creating a system that is equally accessible to all for assessing claims for exemptions to otherwise applicable regulatory rules and instead apply these rules (and the penalties their violation entails) without exception,

but at the same time

(2) an expert (who could reasonably claim an exemption if a system for assessing such claims existed) does not herself have moral reason to abide by those regulatory rules given her special abilities or circumstances.

To resolve this worry, we must show that the state's reasons in (1) can somehow carry over to affect the individual actor's reasons in (2). How should we bridge that gap?

Simester (2021) suggests that cost considerations might help here. As was noted earlier, the 'accommodating D's claim [for an exemption] deprives others of the resources that are needlessly used up by D' (242). If the individual has reasons not to deplete the public purse, then this could be one way to bridge the gap between (1) and (2). Of course, it is not always clear that the cost of setting up a system to adjudicate claims for exemptions would be so large as to *significantly* preclude public spending on other worthwhile aims (particularly given the possibility of financing state activities through additional borrowing). As long as the cost of accommodating D's claim for exemption does not effectively undermine the pursuit of other worthwhile aims or plunge the state into significant debt, then it seems cost considerations might not always be able bridge this gap between (1) and (2).

Still, there can be other reasons why it is not practically feasible to establish a system for assessing requests for exemptions to an otherwise applicable rule, which is equally open to all. Here are some possibilities.

*Political unfeasibility*: perhaps political dysfunction makes it practically impossible to pass the legislation needed to establish such a system for assessing requests for exemptions.

*Lack of expertise*: perhaps establishing such a system in some context requires technical expertise which is unavailable in the jurisdiction for contingent reasons.

*Reduced compliance*: perhaps empirical research in the context at issue shows that adding a system of exemptions would lead to reduced compliance with the generally applicable rules. Maybe introducing exceptions would signal that the values underlying these rules are less clear and compelling, and therefore less binding.

*Risk of abuse by sophisticated parties*: perhaps well-financed companies would use the exemption process to aggressively push for exemptions to costly requirements to increase profitability. This might result in an intolerable level of false positives – exemptions granted although undeserved on safety grounds.

These are just examples of how it might prove unworkable to establish a process for assessing requests for exemptions. Whether any such reasons apply depends on the case. Still, the point is that such considerations help bridge the gap between (1) and (2). These considerations (where applicable) can help explain why an individual expert's desired exemption to the generally applicable rule cannot in fact be granted and thus why it would be unreasonable to claim the exemption nonetheless.

Behind this strategy lies the thought that one's moral obligations are subject to a kind of public defensibility constraint: if one's proposed conduct cannot be publicly justified in ways that would be expected to resonate with everyone (at least everyone engaging rationally and in good faith), then this conduct cannot be deemed permissible. In short, one must be able to justify one's actions in a (reasonable and fair) public setting for them to count as morally permitted.

This thought resembles Scanlon's contractualist view of moral wrongness. He takes it that for our actions to be morally permissible, they must be publicly justifiable to others. More precisely, 'an act is wrong if its performance under the circumstances would be disallowed by any set of principles for the general regulation of behaviour that no one could reasonably reject as a basis for informed, unforced general agreement' (Scanlon 1998: 153). One need not accept the details of Scanlon's view to find some sort of public justifiability criterion of moral permissibility to be plausible in general.

Such a view would help bridge the gap in Simester's argument. Return to Rhea, who performed the malum prohibitum of disposing of hazardous waste without the required licence. Simester's argument, in effect, was that this conduct was indeed morally wrongful (despite being perfectly safe) because Rhea cannot reasonably claim an exemption from the generally applicable licensing requirement, since the opportunity for such exemptions could not (we are assuming) be offered to everyone on an equal basis here. Suppose this is for a combination of the reasons gestured at already: increased cost, political hurdles and reduced compliance with the regulatory scheme in general. The worry for Simester's argument was that it was not obvious why (setting aside her wish not to get in trouble) Rhea should care about the state's reasons for not being able to create a universally available system for requesting an exemption. But we have an answer if we take public justifiability to be a criterion of moral permissibility. Because of the state's reasons in (1) – the practical impossibility of creating a fair and equal system of assessing requests for exemptions – Rhea would not be able to publicly defend her chosen course of conduct (violating the licence requirement) to everyone else. It amounts to claiming for herself a special form of treatment (freedom from the licensing requirement based on personal expertise) that cannot be offered to everyone on an equal basis under the circumstances. If we agree public justifiability is a criterion of moral permissibility, then her act of violating the licence requirement would indeed be morally wrong. If so, then (2) – what Rhea morally should do – aligns with what it is legitimate for the state to do, as described in (1).

If sound, this line of thinking would resolve the malum prohibitum puzzle at least for cases like Rhea's. We sought to show how mala prohibita offences can be consistent with the wrongness constraint in cases like Rhea's. This was a core example where the actor's violation of the malum prohibitum rule seemed not to be morally wrong. But now we have a way to show why her conduct really is morally wrong under the circumstances. Rhea is not in a position to publicly defend her chosen conduct to other members of society. In doing this conduct, she opens herself up to criticism for laying claim to special treatment for herself that cannot be given to others. Hence, Rhea's conduct fails the public justifiability test for moral permissibility. Thus, this malum prohibitum offence does not violate the wrongness constraint on closer inspection.

One might object that this argument about public justifiability only shows that Rhea would be wrong to *request* or *seek* an exemption to the licensing requirement, but not that violating the requirement is itself morally wrong. We disagree. If it is indeed justifiable for the state not to offer Rhea an exemption on the basis that it cannot feasibly be offered on an equal basis to all, and that Rhea therefore cannot publicly justify insisting on giving herself such an exemption, then this implies that Rhea, in fairness, should be subjected to the licensing requirement just like everyone else. Accordingly, it would be wrongful for her to engage in this conduct (violating the licensing requirement), which she cannot reasonably justify to others.

Still, the argument we have been pursuing only goes so far. It does not demonstrate a general obligation to obey any and every justified law that is passed. The argument would not cover mala prohibita that are not part of justified regulatory regimes or where it really *is* reasonably possible for the government to establish processes for evaluating claims for exemptions in a way that is equally open to all. That was assumed not to be the case in the example of Rhea. But if it *were* practically feasible for the state to offer the sought-after special treatment on an equal basis to everybody, then perhaps someone *could* publicly defend her performance of a particular malum prohibitum offence. For example, it might be reasonably possible to accommodate some forms of conscientious objection or religious exemption in a range of cases.[85] If so, the public justifiability criterion would not entail that violating the malum prohibitum on such grounds is wrongful. So, in such a case, we can say that the malum prohibitum offence is over-broad and therefore conflicts with the wrongness constraint (at least where violating the rule cannot be shown to be morally wrong via any of the other arguments discussed in this section).

## 4.4 Conclusion

This section looked at some major theories seeking to reconcile mala prohibita with the wrongness constraint by arguing that it is indeed morally wrongful to commit the proscribed conduct. We looked at traditional theories like consent, fair play and Rawls' natural duty to support just institutions, plus more sophisticated ones that combine elements from the traditional theories (e.g. Wellman's Samaritanism).

In our view, one of the most sophisticated views is Duff's 'civic responsibility' approach. On this view, properly accounting for the wrongfulness of mala prohibita involves defending an underlying political theory that (1) outlines the kinds of civic responsibilities that we have towards fellow citizens (and their limits), and (2) the role of public deliberation in giving them concrete content. When fully fleshed out, these responsibilities might generate moral obligations not to commit many mala prohibita. However, we saw this is a demanding strategy, since it requires establishing nothing short of a full political theory to flesh out our civic responsibilities and how public deliberation helps to determine them.

---

[85] Does the present point carry implications for civil disobedience and whistleblowing? We think not, since it is not clear civil disobedients and whistle-blowers are seeking legal exemptions to begin with.

Accordingly, we offered a less demanding view, building on Simester's arguments, on which it is morally wrong to commit a malum prohibitum if one cannot publicly justify doing so. This offers another route, which could complement a view like Duff's, to account for the wrongfulness of mala prohibita in certain core cases.

## 5 Conclusion

This Element has been concerned with the puzzle of how to reconcile the moral prerequisites of the criminal law, chiefly the wrongness constraint on criminalisation, with mala prohibita offences. These are actions purporting to be wrongful not because of their inherent immorality independent of law, but because of what the law says – where the content or operation of law figures centrally in explaining why the conduct is purportedly wrongful. Particularly where an especially skillful, careful or responsible actor can perform the malum prohibitum offence in a way that is certain not to bring about the harms or risks that the offence was created to combat, one might wonder how there could be any moral wrongness present that would license the criminalisation and punishment of this conduct. If such cases are common, many mala prohibita offences would seem to conflict with the wrongness constraint.

Accordingly, we explored several ways to resolve this tension. One was to abandon the wrongness constraint. Thus, in Section 2, we explored the costs that this would plausibly entail. Most seriously, we found, it would mean the criminal law would lose its ability to credibly and persuasively speak in a moral voice in condemning behaviour that society deems to be beyond the pale. This, in turn, would mean losing a range of attendant benefits that flow from the perceived moral legitimacy of the criminal law – particularly its ability to help inculcate norms within society and increase voluntary compliance with the law to further reduce harm. Although we need not have pursued our policy aims through an institution that condemns misconduct in a moral voice, in fact there is reason to think that common law systems do have such an institution in the criminal law. And given that we do have such an institution, it is important that the condemnatory claims made through criminalisation and conviction are not false or misleading, as this would tend to undermine the perceived legitimacy of our actual institution of criminal justice. Abandoning the wrongness constraint would remove an important safeguard against weakening the power and efficacy of the moral voice of the criminal law.

Section 3 therefore went on to investigate whether mala prohibita offences themselves should yield when they conflict with the wrongness constraint. However, we observed that abandoning mala prohibita would carry important costs as well, especially in losing the practical benefits they offer for advancing legitimate regulatory goals. These benefits include the increased ease of detection and prosecution offered by mala prohibita and their enhanced clarity and ability to guide conduct.

This led us to pose an important background question: how radically would the criminal law have to be revised if we were to rigorously insist on the wrongness constraint? We saw that perhaps it would not end up requiring such radical revisions after all. The reason was that, even assuming many existing mala prohibita offences do conflict with the wrongness constraint, there are several ways to amend the law to remove the conflict besides simply deleting the problematic mala prohibita offences from the criminal code. Instead, we could render them compatible with the wrongness constraint by narrowing the scope of the offence elements or expanding the applicable defences (although the latter strategy seems riskier in making it likelier that more citizens would be haled into court to answer for their conduct even if ultimately acquitted). Thus, we concluded Section 3 by asking whether rigorously applying the wrongness constraint might not entail wholesale removal of so very many offences after all.

This conclusion was bolstered by the discussion of Section 4, where we explored the third and final response to the malum prohibitum puzzle: namely, to provide substantive arguments that many mala prohibita offences, despite first appearances, in fact *do* involve moral wrongs of the sort that would satisfy the wrongness constraint. We looked at several arguments purporting to show that, under some core circumstances, it genuinely is morally wrongful to engage in conduct that is malum prohibitum. These arguments proceeded from a range of different normative principles, including: (1) consent (both explicit and tacit consent), (2) fair play, (3) Rawls' natural duty to support just institutions, (4) the civic responsibilities that citizens owe one another and (5) the idea that one's actions must be publicly defensible to be morally permissible. We investigated the drawbacks of each, as well as more sophisticated views that draw on more than one principle (e.g. Wellman's Samaritanism). However, perhaps through a combination of all these different strategies, the prospects might appear promising for being able to render much malum prohibitum conduct compatible with the wrongness constraint in the end.

Sections 3 and 4, taken together, thus give reason to think that at least some, perhaps many, mala prohibita survive their meeting with the wrongness constraint, even rigorously applied. After all, for any malum prohibitum offence that might seem to conflict with the wrongness constraint, the arguments surveyed in Section 4 provide a recipe for how to argue that on closer inspection this offence does involve a moral wrong (though this must be evaluated on a case-by-case basis). Moreover, even if the arguments of Section 4 do come up short, Section 3 drew our attention to less radical legislative fixes short of eliminating the offending malum prohibitum wholesale from the lawbooks.

In closing, consider one final legislative fix, which offers interesting benefits while carrying novel challenges. We saved this for last because it requires amending the wrongness constraint in certain ways and because it focuses on the law in practice rather than the law on the books (which has been our focus thus far). Specifically, Duff (2018: 67) has argued for a 'de minimis' principle, which can further alleviate the conflict between mala prohibita and a version of the wrongness constraint. A principle of this sort in fact exists in the Model Penal Code, which is the basis for many US state criminal codes.[86] This principle states:

> **De Minimis Provision (DMP):** The Court shall dismiss a prosecution if, having regard to the nature of the conduct charged [and] attendant circumstances, it finds that the defendant's conduct ... did not actually cause or threaten the harm or evil sought to be prevented by the law defining the offence or did so only to an extent too trivial to warrant the condemnation of conviction. (Duff 2018: 67)

This principle would provide a safety valve that courts could apply ex post to resolve any remaining tension between an over-broad malum prohibitum offence – as in cases involving especially skilled actors like Rhea (discussed in Sections 1 and 4) – while still ensuring that society in general can obtain the practical benefits of mala prohibita offences. Duff emphasises that DMP is *not* meant to function as an affirmative defence, which the defendant is responsible for raising. After all, it is not a justification or excuse that denies or mitigates the defendant's misconduct or her culpability therefor. Instead, DMP enables the *court* to act of its own accord to dismiss criminal charges where the conduct technically violates the applicable statute but does not, in the court's estimation, substantially threaten the underlying harm or evil that the statute seeks to combat. This would allow the justice system to maintain the benefits of clear and simple – if potentially over-broad – offence definitions, while helping to avoid unjust convictions in cases where the defendant does not morally deserve it.[87]

If DMP is to reduce the tension between the wrongness constraint and mala prohibita, the wrongness constraint itself must be amended. As formulated earlier, it constrains the law on the books: the applicable offence definitions subject to affirmative defences. The constraint held that the substance of the criminal law must not permit conviction for actions that on balance are morally permissible or else the constraint is violated. But DMP does not alter the law on

---

[86] Model Penal Code § 2.12.    [87] For more on DMP, see Bero and Sarch 2020; Duff 2018: 69.

the books. It does not narrow the scope of offence definitions or broaden the defences. Instead, it gives courts discretion to dismiss charges it deems to pose only de minimis threats to the underlying values and interests to be protected by the relevant law. Thus, DMP leaves the law on the books (i.e. the substance of criminal law rules) unaltered and instead, as Duff acknowledges, seeks to improve the *law in action* (i.e. how it is applied in practice). Thus, if DMP is to help resolve tension between mala prohibita offences and the wrongness constraint, the constraint would have to be amended so it applies not to the laws on the books but the law in action (the case outcomes reached). Specifically, it would have to say that the law in action must not permit convicting defendants for actions that are on balance morally permissible. Duff may be right that case outcomes matter most, but it is also worth asking whether in addition a wrongness constraint that limits the substance of the criminal law (the law on the books) should also be maintained. After all, the law on the books also carries communicative messages about what conduct is deemed sufficiently bad to be worthy of criminalisation. However, DMP would not reduce the tension between a version of the constraint that applies to the law on the books, which has been our concern in previous sections, and over-broad mala prohibita offences.

In addition, beyond this concern, Duff recognises that DMP may also have more substantive drawbacks, including the difficulties of applying such a comparably abstract and vague principle, and that DMP 'accords considerable discretion to prosecutors and other enforcement officials' (Duff 2018: 69). One might fear that such a broad grant of discretion could have worrisome conse-quences, perhaps privileging some socio-economic, political or racial groups over others through conscious or unconscious bias – though the extent to which one shares this worry will likely track one's background level of trust in the judiciary to begin with. Furthermore, one may also worry that DMP could incentivise legislators to be sloppier in drafting offence definitions, since this safety valve could potentially help alleviate problems of over-breadth ex post. Additionally, DMP may also raise separation of powers concerns by delegating too much legislative-style discretion to actors normally tasked with enforcing and applying the law.[88]

Nonetheless, DMP is an intriguing way in which any residual conflict between mala prohibita and the concerns underlying the wrongness constraint might be massaged to a point we are able to live with. In combination, the legislative moves sketched here provide a promising recipe for how we might be able to have our cake and eat it too: to continue our widespread usage of mala

---

[88] For more on these issues, see Bero and Sarch 2020: 409–15.

prohibita offences to obtain their significant practical benefits while insisting on the wrongness constraint to avoid the substantial injustice in convicting actors who have done no moral wrong. This means, of course, that more careful work is required of legislative drafters who author criminal provisions of a malum prohibitum variety and they must be entrusted to make use of the legislative fixes available. But when it is a matter of avoiding injustice and preserving the honesty and integrity of the criminal law, a little extra work seems worth it. We remain cautiously optimistic that legislators are up to the challenge.

# References

Abbott, Ryan and Alex Sarch (2019). 'Punishing Artificial Intelligence: Legal Fiction or Science Fiction?', *UC Davis Law Review* 53: 323–84.

Berman, Mitchell (2012). 'The Justification of Punishment', in *The Routledge Companion to Philosophy of Law*, ed. Andrei Marmor, pp. 141–57, New York: Routledge.

Bero, Steve and Alex Sarch (2020). 'The Problem of Over-Inclusive Offenses: A Closer Look at Duff on Legal Moralism and Mala Prohibita', *Criminal Law and Philosophy* 14: 395–416.

Buell, Samuel (2011). 'What Is Securities Fraud?', *Duke Law Journal* 61: 548–61.

Cahill, Michael (2011). 'Punishment Pluralism', in *Retributivism: Essays on Theory and Policy*, ed. Mark D. White, p. 25–48, New York: Oxford University Press.

Chase, Mike (2019). *How to Become a Federal Criminal*, New York: Atria Books.

Chiao, Vincent (2018). *Criminal Law in the Age of the Administrative State*, Oxford: Oxford University Press.

Coleman, Jules (1992). *Risks and Wrongs*, New York: Oxford University Press.

Cornford, Andrew (2017). 'Rethinking the Wrongness Constraint on Criminalisation', *Law and Philosophy* 36(6): 615–49.

Dagger, Richard (1997). *Civic Virtues: Rights, Citizenship, and Republican Liberalism*, Oxford: Oxford University Press.

Dagger, Richard (2016). 'Crime, Morality, and Republicanism', in *The Routledge Handbook of Criminal Justice Ethics*, ed. Jonathan Jackson and Jonathan Jacobs, pp. 42–57, New York: Routledge.

Darwall, Stephen (2006). *The Second Person Standpoint*, Cambridge, MA: Harvard University Press.

Dimock, Susan (2014). 'Contractarian Criminal Law Theory and *Mala Prohibita* Offences', in *Criminalisation: The Political Morality of the Criminal Law*, ed. R. A. Duff, Lindsay Farmer, Sandra E. Marshall, Massimo Renzo and Victor Tadros, pp. 151–81, Oxford: Oxford University Press.

Dimock, Susan (2016). 'The Malum Prohibitum–Malum In Se Distinction and the Wrongfulness Constraint on Criminalization', *Dialogue: Canadian Philosophical Review* 55: 9–32.

Du Bois-Pedain, Antje (2014). 'The Wrongfulness Constraint in Criminalisation', *Criminal Law and Philosophy* 8: 149–69.

Duff, R. A. (2003). *Punishment, Communication, and Community*, Oxford: Oxford University Press.

Duff, R. A. (2018). *The Realm of Criminal Law*, Oxford: Oxford University Press.

Dworkin, Ronald (1998). *Law's Empire*, 1st ed., Oxford: Hart Publishing.

Edmundson, W. A. (2004). 'State of the Art: The Duty to Obey the Law', *Legal Theory* 10(4): 215–59.

Edwards, James (2017). 'Criminalisation without Punishment', *Legal Theory* 23(2): 69–95.

Edwards, James and Andrew Simester (2017). 'What's Public About Crime?' *Oxford Journal of Legal Studies* 37(1): 105–33.

Enoch, David (2014). 'Authority and Reason-Giving', *Philosophy and Phenomenological Research* 89(2): 296–332.

Feinberg, Joel (1965). 'The Expressive Function of Punishment', *The Monist* 49 (3): 397–423.

Feinberg Joel (1984). *Harm to Others: The Moral Limits of the Criminal Law*, New York: Oxford University Press.

Feldman, Fred (2006). 'Actual Utility, the Objection from Impracticality, and the Move to Expected Utility', *Philosophical Studies* 129: 49–79.

Gardner, George K. (1953). 'Bailey v. Richardson and the Constitution of the United States', *Boston University Law Review* 33: 176–203.

Gardner, John (2007). *Offences and Defences*, Oxford: Oxford University Press.

Gardner, John (2020). *Torts and Other Wrongs*, Oxford: Oxford University Press.

Goldberg, John and Ben Zipursky (2020). *Recognizing Wrongs*, Cambridge, MA: Harvard University Press.

Green, Stuart (1971). 'Why It's a Crime to Tear the Tag Off a Mattress: Overcriminalization and the Moral Content of Regulatory Offenses', *Emory Law Journal* 46: 1533–616.

Green, Stuart (1997). 'Why It's a Crime to Tear the Tag Off a Mattress', *Emory Law Journal* 46: 1533–1615.

Green, Stuart (2006). *Lying, Stealing, and Cheating: A Moral Theory of White-Collar Crime*, Oxford: Oxford University Press.

Hamdani, Assaf (2007). 'Mens Rea and the Cost of Ignorance', *Virginia Law Review* 93: 415–57.

Hart, H. L. A. (1955). 'Are There Any Natural Rights?' *The Philosophical Review* 64(2): 175–91.

Hart, H. L. A. (2008). *Punishment and Responsibility*, 2nd ed., Oxford: Oxford University Press.

Hershovitz, Scott (2011). 'Corrective Justice for Civil Recourse Theorists', *Florida State Law Review* 39: 107–28.

Hershovitz, Scott (2012). 'The Authority of Law', in *The Routledge Companion to Philosophy of Law*, ed. Andrei Marmor, pp. 65–76, New York: Routledge.

Hershovitz, Scott (2017). 'Treating Wrongs as Wrongs: An Expressive Argument for Tort Law', *Journal of Tort Law* 10: 1–43.

Horton, John (2010). *Political Obligation*, 2nd ed., Basingstoke: Palgrave Macmillan.

Hoskins, Zachary (2019). *Beyond Punishment? A Normative Account of the Collateral Legal Consequences of Conviction*, New York: Oxford University Press.

Hume, David (1752). 'Of the Original Contract', https://cpb-us-w2.wpmucdn .com/blogs.cofc.edu/dist/8/406/files/2014/09/David-Hume-Of-the-Original-Contract-1kif9ud.pdf.

Husak, Douglas (2004). 'The Criminal Law as Last Resort', *Oxford Journal of Legal Studies* 24: 207–35.

Husak, Douglas (2005). 'Malum Prohibitum and Retributivism', in *Defining Crimes: Essays on The Special Part of the Criminal Law*, ed. R. A. Duff and Stuart Green, pp. 65–90, Oxford: Oxford University Press.

Husak, Douglas (2008). *Overcriminalization: The Limits of the Criminal Law*, Oxford: Oxford University Press.

Husak, Douglas (2016). *Ignorance of Law*, New York: Oxford University Press.

Husak, Douglas (2020). 'The Price of Criminal Law Skepticism: Ten Functions of the Criminal Law', *New Criminal Law Review* 23(1): 27–59.

Kaplow, Louis and Steven Shavell (2002). *Fairness versus Welfare*, Cambridge, MA: Harvard University Press.

Klosko, George (2005). *Political Obligations*, Oxford: Oxford University Press.

Kramer, Matthew (2005). 'Legal and Moral Obligation', in *The Blackwell Guide to the Philosophy of Law and Legal Theory*, ed. Martin Golding and William Edmundson, pp. 179–90, Oxford: Blackwell Publishing.

Lee, Ambrose Y. K. (2015). 'Public Wrongs and the Criminal Law', *Criminal Law and Philosophy* 9: 155–70.

Lee, Youngjae (2021). '*Mala Prohibita* and Proportionality', *Criminal Law and Philosophy* 15: 425–46.

Lee, Youngjae (2022a). '*Mala Prohibita*, the Wrongfulness Constraint, and the Problem of Overcriminalization', *Law and Philosophy*, 41: 375–96.

Lee, Youngjae (2022b). 'Proxy Crimes and Overcriminalization', *Criminal Law and Philosophy* 16: 469–484.

Lefkowitz, David (2006). 'The Duty to Obey the Law', *Philosophy Compass* 1(6): 571–98.

Locke, John (1980 [1690]). *John Locke: Second Treatise of Government*, ed. C. B. McPherson, Indianapolis IN: Hackett Publishing.

Mill, John Stuart (2003 [1859]). *On Liberty.* London: Penguin.

Mill, John Stuart (2004 [1861]). *Utilitarianism.* London: Penguin.

Moore, Michael (1997). *Placing Blame: A Theory of Criminal Law*, Oxford: Oxford University Press.

Nozick, Robert (1974). *Anarchy, State, and Utopia*, Malden, MA: Blackwell Publishing.

Rawls, John (1971). *A Theory of Justice*, Cambridge, MA: Harvard University Press.

Raz, Joseph (1979). *The Authority of Law*, Oxford: Oxford University Press.

Raz, Joseph (1994). 'The Obligation to Obey: Revision and Tradition', in *Ethics in the Public Domain: Essays in the Morality of Law and Politics*, pp. 341–54, Oxford: Clarendon Press.

Ristroph, Alice (2011a). 'Responsibility for the Criminal Law' in *Philosophical Foundations of Criminal Law*, ed. R. A. Duff and Stuart Green, pp. 107–14, Oxford: Oxford University Press.

Ristroph, Alice (2011b). 'Criminal Law in the Shadow of Violence', *Alabama Law Review* 62: 571–621.

Robinson, Paul (1996). 'The Criminal-Civil Distinction and the Utility of Desert', *Boston University Law Review* 76: 201–14.

Robinson, Paul and John Darley (1995). *Justice, Liability & Blame: Community Views and the Criminal Law*, Boulder, CO: Westview Press.

Robinson, Paul and John Darley (2014). *The Utility of Desert: The Structure and Limits of Criminal Law*, New York: Routledge.

Scanlon, Thomas M. (1998). *What We Owe to Each Other*, Cambridge, MA: Harvard University Press.

Simester, Andrew P. (2021). *Fundamentals of Criminal Law*, Oxford: Oxford University Press.

Simester, Andrew P. (2012). 'Prophylactic Crimes', in *Seeking Security: Pre-Empting the Commission of Criminal Harms*, ed. G. R. Sullivan and Ian Dennis, pp. 59–78, Oxford: Hart.

Simester, Andrew. P. and Andreas von Hirsch (2011). *Crimes, Harms and Wrongs*, Oxford: Hart.

Simmons, A. John (1976). 'Tacit Consent and Political Obligation', *Philosophy and Public Affairs* 5(3): 274–91.

Simmons, A. John (1979). 'The Principle of Fair Play', *Philosophy and Public Affairs* 8(4): 307–37.

Simmons, A. John (1981). *Moral Principles and Political Obligations*, Princeton: Princeton University Press.

Simmons, A. John (1987). 'The Anarchist Position: A Reply to Klosko and Senor', *Philosophy and Public Affairs* 16(3): 269–79.

Simmons, A. John (2001). *Justification and Legitimacy*, Cambridge: Cambridge University Press.

Smith, M. B. E. (1973). 'Is There a Prima Facie Obligation to Obey the Law?' *Yale Law Journal* 82(5): 950–76.

Tadros, Victor (2012). 'Wrongness and Criminalization' in *The Routledge Companion to Philosophy of Law*, ed. Andrei Marmor, pp. 157–73, New York: Routledge.

The Law Commission (2010). 'Criminal Liability in Regulatory Contexts', Consultation Paper No. 195, www.lawcom.gov.uk/app/uploads/2015/06/cp195_Criminal_Liability_consultation.pdf.

Viehoff, Daniel (2014). 'Democratic Equality and Political Authority', *Philosophy and Public Affairs* 42(4): 337–75.

Walen, Alec (2020). 'Criminal Law and Penal Law: The Wrongness Constraint and a Complementary Forfeiture Model', *Criminal Law and Philosophy* 14: 431–46.

Wellman, Christopher H. (2001). 'Toward a Liberal Theory of Political Obligation', *Ethics* 111(4): 735–59.

Wellman, Christopher H. (2013). 'Rights Forfeiture and Mala Prohibita', in *The Constitution of the Criminal Law*, ed. R. A. Duff, Lindsay Farmer, S. E. Marshall, Massimo Renzo and Victor Tadros, pp. 77–96, Oxford: Oxford University Press.

Wellman, Christopher H. and A. John Simmons (2005). 'Natural Duties and the Duty to Obey the Law', in *Is There a Duty to Obey the Law?*, pp. 121–88, Cambridge: Cambridge University Press.

Zimmerman, Michael. (2002). 'Taking Luck Seriously', *The Journal of Philosophy* 99(11): 553–76.

# Cambridge Elements ☰

# Philosophy of Law

## Series Editors

### George Pavlakos
*University of Glasgow*

George Pavlakos is Professor of Law and Philosophy at the School of Law, University of Glasgow. He has held visiting posts at the universities of Kiel and Luzern, the European University Institute, the UCLA Law School, the Cornell Law School and the Beihang Law School in Beijing. He is the author of *Our Knowledge of the Law* (2007) and more recently has co-edited *Agency, Negligence and Responsibility* (2021) and *Reasons and Intentions in Law and Practical Agency* (2015).

### Gerald J. Postema
*University of North Carolina at Chapel Hill*

Gerald J. Postema is Professor Emeritus of Philosophy at the University of North Carolina at Chapel Hill. Among his publications count *Utility, Publicity, and Law: Bentham's Moral and Legal Philosophy* (2019); *On the Law of Nature, Reason, and the Common Law: Selected Jurisprudential Writings of Sir Matthew Hale* (2017); *Legal Philosophy in the Twentieth Century: The Common Law World* (2011), *Bentham and the Common Law Tradition*, 2nd edition (2019).

### Kenneth M. Ehrenberg
*University of Surrey*

Kenneth M. Ehrenberg is Professor of Jurisprudence and Philosophy at the University of Surrey School of Law and Co-Director of the Surrey Centre for Law and Philosophy. He is the author of *The Functions of Law* (2016) and numerous articles on the nature of law, jurisprudential methodology, the relation of law to morality, practical authority, and the epistemology of evidence law.

## Associate Editor

### Sally Zhu
*University of Sheffield*

Sally Zhu is a lecturer in property law at the University of Sheffield. Her research is on property and private law aspects of platform and digital economies.

## About the Series

This series provides an accessible overview of the philosophy of law, drawing on its varied intellectual traditions in order to showcase the interdisciplinary dimensions of jurisprudential enquiry, review the state of the art in the field, and suggest fresh research agendas for the future. Focusing on issues rather than traditions or authors, each contribution seeks to deepen our understanding of the foundations of the law, ultimately with a view to offering practical insights into some of the major challenges of our age.

Cambridge Elements ≡

# Philosophy of Law

## Elements in the Series

A full series listing is available at: www.cambridge.org/EPHL

Printed in the United States
by Baker & Taylor Publisher Services